IS FOR PELOTON

AN A-Z OF CYCLING

SUZE CLEMITSON
& MARK FAIRHURST

BLOOMSBURY

LONDON · NEW DELHI · NEW YORK · SYDNEY

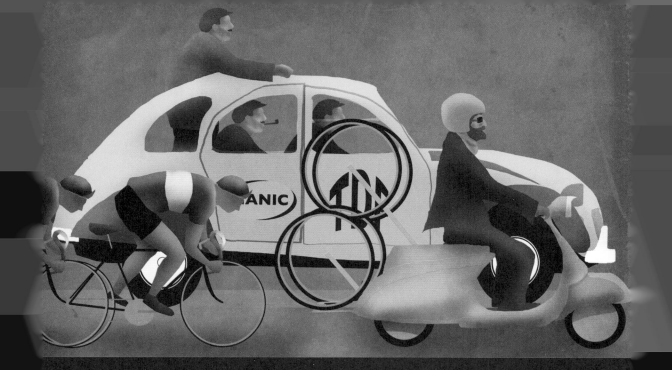

BLOOMSBURY SPORT
An imprint of Bloomsbury Publishing Plc

50 Bedford Square   1385 Broadway
London   New York
WC1B 3DP   NY 10018
UK   USA

www.bloomsbury.com

BLOOMSBURY and the Diana logo are
trademarks of Bloomsbury Publishing Plc

First published 2015

© Suze Clemitson and Mark Fairhurst, 2015
Illustrations © Mark Fairhurst, 2015

Suze Clemitson and Mark Fairhurst
have asserted their right under the
Copyright, Designs and Patents Act, 1988,
to be identified as Author and Illustrator
of this work

British Library Cataloguing-in-
Publication Data

A catalogue record for this book is
available from the British Library.

Library of Congress Cataloguing-in-
Publication data has been applied for.

ISBN: HB: 978-1-4729-1285-5
        ePDF: 978-1-4729-2419-3
        ePub: 978-1-4729-1286-2

2 4 6 8 10 9 7 5 3 1

Designed by Austin Taylor
Printed and bound in China by C&C Offset
   Printing Co

Bloomsbury Publishing Plc makes every
effort to ensure that the papers used in
the manufacture of our books are natural
recyclable products made from wood
grown in well-managed forests. Our
manufacturing processes conform to the
environmental regulations of the country
of origin.

To find out more about our authors and
books visit www.bloomsbury.com. Here you
will find extracts, author interviews, details
of forthcoming events and the option to
sign up for our newsletters.

EVER SINCE THE FIRST TOUR DE FRANCE, CYCLE RACING has captured the imagination of millions of people. The drama, passion, pain and glory has been the stuff of legends.

The beauty of cycling is that it knows no barriers. It's classless. Whether you ride a second-hand bicycle or the latest machine featuring the pinnacle in technical development, you are part of an ever-expanding movement that is ecologically low impact and good for you.

It inspires.

Mark Fairhurst's art carries that inspiration. Humorous, thought-provoking, encouraging; his work in this book is a joy to see and have.

Remember, 'P is for Peloton'. Get on your bike and RIDE!

Sir Dave Brailsford

TEAM PRINCIPAL, TEAM SKY

A IS FOR ...

ARRIVÉE

YOU SAY ▸ *A (as in apple) – REE – VAY (rhymes with say)*

WHAT IT MEANS ▸ Let's start at the finish – *Arrivée* is the French word for the finish line of a race, usually marked by a giant inflatable archway. In 2013, the Orica-Greenedge team bus managed to get wedged underneath the finish line at the Tour de France but the *arrivée* is usually the stage for a rider to cross the finish line and throw their arms aloft in the traditional V of victory.

ABANDON

When a rider is forced to climb off his bike during a race because of illness or injury, he 'abandons' and may end up in the broom wagon *(see B)*.

AERODYNAMICS

A cyclist's greatest enemy is wind (no, not that kind). In order to cut through the air with maximum efficiency you need to be as aerodynamic as possible in order to reduce the drag effect that wind creates. Even though you feel you're moving forward, wind drag is always pulling you backwards. Minimising drag is the key for making a cyclist go faster, and cycling teams often spend a significant amount of money sending riders into wind tunnels to measure how aerodynamic they are. There are several key factors to making a cyclist more aerodynamically efficient:

Clothing – Team Sky have popularised the use of skinsuits for time trials, where aerodynamics are of huge importance, with individual cyclists riding alone against the clock, with no rider or peloton in front to take the brunt of the wind. Imagine going swimming fully clothed and the effort you need to expend to get through the water; the same is true of a cyclist passing through air; if less immediately appreciable. This is the reason cyclists wear clothing that's as streamlined and form-fitting as possible.

Aero bars and helmet – aero bars protrude straight out from the front of the bike and you can rest your entire forearm on them and lie flatter on the bike,

which helps to shrink the 'wall' your body presents to the wind in front: less wind slams into your body, and more flows over. Aero helmets work by smoothing the shape your head makes and improving airflow around it and make a significant time saving in a time trial – a small price for looking like an alien.

Position – this is the biggest single factor in the rider-plus-bike-versus-wind equation, as a cyclist's body accounts for 70–80 per cent of drag. The bigger you are,

CONTINUED OVERLEAF ▶

AERODYNAMICS

the higher that percentage goes, which is why so many of today's professional cyclists are so skinny, giving them a far better power to weight ratio and better aerodynamics. The rule is: the flatter you can get on the bike, the better. Get into a good aerodynamic tuck and you'll scythe through the air like a Cavendish or a Wiggins – or you'll go faster, anyway.

BLUFF FACT ► In the decisive time trial at the end of the 1989 Tour de France, Greg LeMond used aero bars and an aero helmet. If Laurent Fignon had worn a cap he would have won the Tour.

ALLEZ!

YOU SAY ► *AL (rhyme with pal) – AY (rhymes with hey!)*

WHAT IT MEANS ► Go! Come on! *Allez* is the universal expression of cycling encouragement, shouted from French roadsides since 1868 when Englishman James Moore won a 1200-metre race on 31 May 1868 at the Parc de Saint-Cloud, Paris. Equivalents include *vai* in Italian and *venga* in Spanish. Somewhat bizarrely, the Dutch and Belgian fans shout '*hop*' at their riders.

ALPE D'HUEZ

YOU SAY ► *ALP – DOO – EZ (rhymes with fez)*
ALTITUDE ► 1850 metres
HEIGHT GAIN ► 1150 metres
AVERAGE GRADIENT ► 8 per cent
MAXIMUM GRADIENT ► 13 per cent
LENGTH ► 14.5 kilometres
LOCATION ► French Alps

The Alpe d'Huez is probably the most famous mountain climb in cycling and certainly the most glamorous in the Tour de France, where it was the scene of the first ever mountaintop finish in the race. First climbed in 1952, its 21 hairpins (or *lacets*) loop their way from the village of Bourg-d'Oisans to the ski resort at the summit. Your prize for winning the stage? Your name on a sign at one of those famous *lacets*. Fausto Coppi's name is there – he was the first to win on the Alpe. Lance Armstrong's name is not, though he won there twice – the Alpe doesn't acknowledge some of its miscreants. Christophe Riblon is the most recent winner – in 2013 he won the historic 'double d'Huez' stage in the Tour de France when the Alpe was climbed twice in the same stage.

The 21 signs on the 21 hairpin bends each bear the names of the riders who have won on the most glamorous mountain in cycling:

1 **GIUSEPPE GUERINI** (1999). The Italian climber was knocked off his bike by a young German photographer – eager to take a photo. Guerini got up, hopped back on his bike and was so far ahead he still won the stage.

2 **MARCO PANTANI** (1997). The pirate won 19 months after an accident at Milan–Turin which would have ended the career of many riders – he suffered multiple compound fractures to his left leg.

3 **MARCO PANTANI** (1995). This is generally agreed to be the record ascent at 37 minutes and 35 seconds, and was Pantani's first stage win in the Tour.

4 **ROBERTO CONTI** (1994). Eros Poli had won the day before on Mont Ventoux and now another gregario had his day. This was 30-year-old Conti's first ever professional win.

5 **ANDY HAMPSTEN** (1992). The first – and now only – American winner on the Alpe.

6 **GIANNI BUGNO** (1991). This was Bugno's second success on the Alpe, and he became the first rider to climb the Alpe in under 40 minutes.

7 **GIANNI BUGNO** (1990). Bugno beat Greg LeMond who would go on to win the Tour.

8 **GERT-JAN THEUNISSE** (1989). The last Dutchman to win here – the Alpe has been known as the Dutch mountain because of the extraordinary success of Dutch climbers. The only man to win on the Alpe in the polka dot jersey.

9 **STEVEN ROOKS** (1988). Another Dutchman.

10 **FREDERICO ECHAVE** (1987). This was the first win on the Alpe by a Spaniard. The Irish are now trying to claim this one as 'Irish Corner'.

11 **BERNARD HINAULT** (1986). Hinault is credited with the win though he and team-mate LeMond crossed the finish line hand in hand at the finish of one of the most iconic stages in Tour de France history.

12 **LUIS HERRERA** (1984). 'Lucho' was riding for the amateur Colombian team.

CONTINUED OVERLEAF ►

13 PETER WINNEN (1983). A double winner, the Dutchman said he felt the climb had taken five years off his life.

14 BEAT BREU (1982). The only Swiss to win on the Alpe, he attacked from the foot of the climb and was never caught.

15 PETER WINNEN (1981). Winnen was in his first year as a professional when he scored his first win on the Alpe.

16 JOOP ZOETEMELK (1979) and Pierre Rolland (2011). In 1979 the Alpe was climbed twice on successive days, Zoetemelk won the second time around. Rolland was only the second Frenchman to win on the Alpe where he sealed the white jersey. 'I know the Alpe by heart' he said afterwards.

17 JOACHIM AGOSTINHO (1979) and Carlos Sastre (2008). Agostinho was the only Portuguese rider to win on the Alpe and was 36 at the time. Sastre won the Tour on this stage with a well-orchestrated attack to take the yellow jersey from his team-mate Frank Schleck.

18 HENNIE KUIPER (1978) and Frank Schleck (2006). Kuiper, yet another Dutchman; and Schleck, the first rider from Luxembourg to win on the Alpe.

19 HENNIE KUIPER (1977). The Dutchman's win from the year before.

20 JOOP ZOETEMELK (1976) and Iban Mayo (2003). In 1976 Dutchman Father Jaap started a tradition with Zoetemelk's win of ringing the church bells for every Dutch victory, which made him a very busy man. The Spaniard Mayo attacked seven kilometres from the summit and won *a la* Pantani, completing the climb in 39 minutes and 6 seconds.

21 FAUSTO COPPI (1952). The Italian's style beat Robic's sheer guts in a classic duel to take the first ever mountaintop finish in the Tour. His time for the first ever ascent was 45 minutes and 52 seconds.

BLUFF IT ▸ *'Frenchman Michel Pollentier actually won on the Alpe in 1978, but he was disqualified for trying to fool the doping control with a condom full of someone else's pee.'*

ANGLIRU

YOU SAY ▸ *ANG (rhymes with hang) – LEE – ROO*
ALTITUDE ▸ 1573 metres
HEIGHT GAIN ▸ 1245 metres
AVERAGE GRADIENT ▸ 10 per cent
MAXIMUM GRADIENT ▸ 24 per cent
LENGTH ▸ 12.2 kilometres
LOCATION ▸ Picos de Europa, Spain

The Alpe d'Huez might be more famous, but the Angliru is one of the hardest climbs ever used in cycling where it forms part of the *Vuelta a España*. The Angliru was originally for goats – not cars or cyclists – and the hardest part is still called 'the Goat Track'. In fact it's so difficult and so steep that some riders just get off and walk. Often compared to Monte Zoncolan in Italy, the Angliru was unknown before 1996 when a member of a Spanish cycling team decided to check out

rumours of a super-steep climb hidden away in the Picos de Europa, the razor sharp mountain range that isolates the Asturias region from the rest of Spain. It was introduced into the Vuelta a España in 1999, and one of the riders who won there, the Spanish climber Roberto Heras, described it simply as 'hell, there's nothing like it'. Abandoning the Vuelta a España in 2002, British rider David Millar shouted 'We're not animals and this is inhuman!' as he refused to cross the finish line. Deceptive in its early kilometres, the Angliru saves its savagery for the last six kilometres, which ramp up to an alarming 13 per cent with the *coup de grâce*, the *Cueña les Cabres*, that infamous goat track, reaching an almost impossible 24 per cent just three kilometres from the summit.

BLUFF IT ▸ *"It would have been impossible to climb the Angliru even 20 years ago, old-fashioned gear ratios were just too high.'*

ARDENNES

The Ardennes, along with the Flanders region in north-west Belgium, have been called the 'beating heart of Belgian cycling'. This wooded and hilly region in southern Belgium is famous for the races known as the Spring Classics, the *Flèche Wallonne* and *Liège–Bastogne–Liège*. The climbs may not have the grandeur of the Alps or the Pyrenees, but they are steep. The Cauberg has a maximum gradient of 12 per cent, la Redoute 17 per cent and the Mur de Huy a whopping 26 per cent. The Mur de Huy really is like climbing a wall. Try doing that on your bike.

ATTACK

When a rider launches himself off the front of the peloton, he goes on the attack. Baroudeurs *(see B)* live for the opportunity to launch a long range bid for glory. For the GC contenders, the mountains are the place where Grand Tours are won and lost, though Hugo Koblet – the '*pedaleur de charme*' – won the 1951 Tour de France by attacking on a flat stage.

BLUFF IT ▸ *'As Bernard Hinault, one of the most aggressive riders ever, used to say: "As long as I breathe, I attack"*

ANQUETIL Jacques

BORN ▸ 8 January, 1934, Mont-Saint-Aignan
(Normandy), France
DIED ▸ 18 November, 1987, Rouen (Normandy), France
NATIONALITY ▸ French
ACTIVE ▸ 1953–1969
RIDER TYPE ▸ All-rounder, Anquetil was a quite
outstanding time triallist
NICKNAMES ▸ *Maître Jacques* (Master Jacques),
Monsieur Chrono (Mr Time Trial)
BIG WINS ▸ 5 × Tour de France (1957, 1961, 1962,
1963, 1964), 2 × Giro d'Italia (1960, 1964), Vuelta
a España (1963), 9 × Grand Prix des Nations
(1953, 1954, 1955, 1956, 1957, 1958, 1961, 1965, 1966),
Liège–Bastogne–Liège (1966), hour record (1956)
MAJOR RIVAL ▸ Raymond Poulidor

Jacques Anquetil was the French rider, born in
Normandy, who became the first man ever to
win the Tour de France five times, taking only eight
years to do so, the first in 1957 with four wins in
a row from 1961 to 1964. He was the first rider to
achieve the Tour de France–Vuelta a España double,
and the first to win all three of the Grand Tours.
He was an excellent all-round rider but his big
strength was time trialling – the Bradley Wiggins of
his day. His intense rivalry with Raymond Poulidor
'the Eternal Second' divided France. Anquetil was
considered to be cold and calculating, though in the
peloton he was as admired for his courteousness
and sense of fair play as Poulidor was disliked for
his bad temper and selfish tactics.

In 1964, their enmity culminated in one of the
most famous stages of the Tour de France when
Anquetil and Poulidor climbed the Puy de Dôme
literally elbow to elbow, with the time triallist
bluffing the climber every pedal stroke of the way,
clinging to him like a limpet. Poulidor, realising
too late that he had been conned, attacked in the
final kilometre and ended the stage only 14
seconds behind his rival, but it was too little
too late. Anquetil's response? 'That's thirteen
seconds more than I need'.

Anquetil was a notorious party animal,
staying up late during races drinking champagne,
but he would do anything to beat Poulidor. After
withdrawing from a race in 1967 owing to the
pulmonary trouble that dogged his career, he was
on a drinking binge with friends when one of
them toasted to Poulidor's anticipated success the
next day. 'Set the alarm for 7' he told his wife. He
was on the start line the next morning and beat
Poulidor yet again.

But it was Anquetil's life off the bike that was
truly bizarre – he was involved in a love triangle
with the wife of his doctor and her step-daughter
for many years, a self-confessed doper and lover of
astronomy and CB radio. He became great friends
with Poulidor, saying that cycling had robbed them
of fifteen years of friendship. Anquetil's love of the
good life finally caught up with him – he was dead
at 53 from stomach cancer. But he never lost his
dry humour, saying on his deathbed 'Raymond,
you're going to finish second again.'

RIDER

ARMSTRONG Lance

BORN ▸ 18 September, 1971, Plano (Texas), United States

NATIONALITY ▸ American

ACTIVE ▸ 1992–2011

RIDER TYPE ▸ All-rounder, strong in the time trials and the mountains

NICKNAMES ▸ The Boss, Big Tex, Mellow Johnny (from *maillot jaune*)

BIG WINS ▸ 7 × Tour de France* (*Armstrong was stripped of his Tour de France titles gained between 1999–2005 in 2012), 1 × world championships (1993), San Sebastián Classic (1995)

MAJOR RIVALS ▸ Jan Ullrich, Marco Pantani

The world now knows, thanks to Oprah Winfrey and the work of the US Anti-Doping Agency, that Lance Armstrong did *not* win a record-breaking seven Tours de France. Even though the world saw him ride up the Champs-Élysées in the yellow jersey seven times, he had used performance-enhancing methods including EPO and blood doping to achieve those victories and they were stripped by the UCI in 2012. All those career-defining moments – the attack on Sestriere in 1999 when he was likened to a motorbike; the 'look' he gave Jan Ullrich on the Alpe d'Huez in 2001; the 'Blue Train' of his US Postal team dominating the 2002 team time trial; the off-road bike handling skills when he avoided the Joseba Beloki crash in 2003 and the recovery from the crash on Luz Ardiden to win the stage and the race in the same year; even his third place comeback in 2007 – all were a product of what the US Anti-Doping Agency called 'the most sophisticated, professionalized and successful doping program that sport has ever seen'.

AUTOBUS

YOU SAY ▸ *OR – TOE – BOOS (rhymes with loose)*

WHAT IT MEANS ▸ This is the large group of riders that forms at the back of the race, usually during the mountain stages. This is where you find the sprinters and the big men, the *domestiques* (see D) who have done their job of shepherding their team leader for the day, the worn out and injured and those who just haven't got the 'legs' that day. Team rivalries are set aside as these riders unite around one common aim – to get to the finish line before they're eliminated for being outside the time limit, which is set at a percentage of the winner's finish time. The other good reason for staying in the *autobus* or *grupetto* is that there's safety in numbers: while the *commissaires* might be happy to exclude one or two riders, they're less happy about excluding a large group, especially if some of the star sprinters are facing the chop.

B IS FOR ...

BICYCLE

Ah, the bicycle – the most efficient vehicle ever invented – and the most environmentally friendly, not to mention the healthiest. This simple, affordable machine can be used for transportation, fun, fitness and sport. The first human powered land vehicle was invented in 1418 but the mountain bike didn't appear until 1977. There are a billion bicycles in the world and 50 million more are manufactured every year. The first real bicycle was the velocipede or boneshaker (1865) – an aptly named wooden machine with metal tyres – then came the penny farthing and then the safety bicycle, popular in the 1880s. This is the prototype for all modern bicycles with its diamond shaped frame, two wheels of equal size and chain driven back wheel. The bicycle has brought more personal and social mobility and a greater sense of liberation to more people than any other invention – no wonder it became known as 'the freedom machine'.

BLUFF FACT ▶ The pneumatic tyre was used on bikes before cars.

BLUFF IT ▶ *'Of course metal wheel rims weren't used in the Tour de France until 1935 – until then they used wooden wheels.'*

BAROUDEUR

YOU SAY ▶ *BAA (like a sheep) – ROO – DUR (rhymes with fur)*
WHAT IT MEANS ▶ Who doesn't love a long, lone breakaway – those plucky underdogs trying, usually hopelessly, to stay away from the speeding peloton? The French have a word for them, and that word is *baroudeur*. It comes from the Arabic, where its meaning is 'dynamite'. The French use it to mean 'adventurer' and in bike racing it's all about the riders who like to put a bomb under the race and go off on the attack.

BLUFF IT ▶ *'Look there's Jens Voigt in the break – he's a typical* baroudeur*'.*

BARTALI Gino

BORN ▸ 18 July, 1914, Florence (Tuscany), Italy
DIED ▸ 5 May, 2000, Florence (Tuscany), Italy
NATIONALITY ▸ Italian
RIDER TYPE ▸ All-rounder with excellent climbing abilities
ACTIVE ▸ 1935–1954
NICKNAMES ▸ The Man of Iron, Gino the Pious
BIG WINS ▸ 2 × Tour de France (1938, 1948), 3 × Giro d'Italia (1936, 1937, 1947), 4 × Milan–San Remo (1939, 1940, 1947, 1950), 7 × king of the mountains at the Giro d'Italia (1935, 1936, 1937, 1939, 1940, 1946, 1947)
MAJOR RIVAL ▸ Fausto Coppi

Gino Bartali holds the record for the longest time between two Tours de France wins, 10 years (1938 and 1948). His performance in the 1938 Tour de France is the stuff of legend and he finished the race as the king of the mountains as well as the yellow jersey, the first time the feat was ever achieved. In 1948 he was credited with helping Italy to avoid civil war by winning again, ten years later (a record never equalled) – it's a legend, but of such legends the Tour de France is made.

Bartali enjoyed such an intense rivalry with Fausto Coppi that the two riders were ordered to sign a peace pact in the 1949 Tour when Coppi made his debut at the race. It started in the 1940 Giro when the young star, newly signed for Bartali's Legano team, decided to win the race himself and the older man ordered his team to ride Coppi down at every opportunity. In the 1948 world championships, both riders abandoned rather than ride to support the other. The pact held in 1949 with Coppi winning and Bartali finishing as runner-up. There was a famous incident in the 1952 Tour when the riders shared a bottle, and even then a dispute raged as to who offered a *bidon* to whom.

One of the greatest riders ever, his greatest achievement didn't happen on the bike. In 2013 he was named 'righteous among the nations' at the Yad Vashem Holocaust Memorial in Jerusalem for his work saving the lives of Italian Jews in the Second World War. Bartali worked as a courier for the Jewish-Christian rescue network in Florence, hiding photographs and forged identity documents in the handlebars and seat post of his bicycle – if stopped and searched he would specifically ask that those parts of his bike be left untouched as they were calibrated for maximum speed. He was responsible for helping a Jewish friend Giacomo Goldenberg and his family to hide in a cellar and supported them throughout the war, despite the enormous risk involved – at one point he was even arrested and questioned by the secret police in Florence. Yet he never spoke about his role as a secret hero, only telling his son: 'If you're good at a sport, they attach the medals to your shirt and then they shine in some museum. That which is earned by doing good deeds is attached to the soul and shines elsewhere.' When people told him he was a hero he would reply 'No, no. I want to be remembered for my sporting achievements. Real heroes are others, those who have suffered in their soul, in their heart, in their spirit, in their mind, for their loved ones. Those are the real heroes. I'm just a cyclist.'

BLUFF IT ▸ *'Years before Nike, Bartali had the words "Just Do It" written in Italian on his cycling cap'.*

B IS FOR...

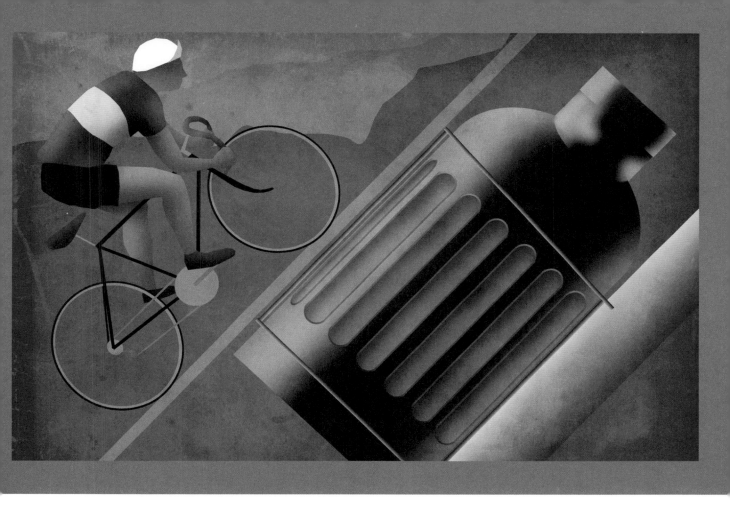

BIDON

YOU SAY ▸ *BEE – DON*

WHAT IS IT? ▸ If you've ever been to a bike race you might have been part of the scramble to grab a plastic drinking bottle tossed to the roadside. These are *bidons* and they're usually branded with sponsors' logos. They make a great souvenir – especially if they came from a Wiggins or a Cavendish. In case you're worried about the ecological impact of all that litter, most races now have designated sections along the route where riders can dispose of their empties.

BLUFF IT ▸ *'I saw rider x stuff 13 bidons up his jersey in two minutes – I believe that's a record.'*

BONIFICATION

Or, more simply, *bonif*. A *bonification* is a time bonus awarded to a rider for winning a stage, an intermediate sprint, or taking the king of the mountains prize on the summit of a climb. Somewhat confusingly, the *bonification* – or bonus – is subtracted from the rider's time, not added to it. For the definitive pronunciation of the word, try listening to Sean Kelly commentating on a bike race.

BONK

See *Fringale*. The bonk is that horrible sinking feeling when your body's energy stores hit 'empty'. Runners call it 'hitting the wall' and it's the moment when you can't go any further and start pedalling squares *(see P)*.

BREAKAWAY

In any race a breakaway will form at some point, often gaining huge time gaps over the main field. On a flat stage, the sprinters' teams will work together to bring back the breakaway using Chapatte's Law. Robert Chapatte, a French ex-professional cyclist turned TV commentator, noticed that a speeding peloton takes 10 kilometres to gain back one minute on a breakaway, though with advances in bike technology and rider fitness it's now more like 90 seconds. His law is so precise that you often see riders caught inside the final kilometres. On a mountain stage you'll see the teams of the main contenders riding a fast tempo on the climbs to keep their riders out of trouble and in contention, but when it comes to a mountaintop finish it's every man for himself. Very occasionally a breakaway gains such a huge advantage that it affects the result of the race – Roger Walkowiak won the Tour de France

in this way in 1956. The longest solo breakaway ever was 315 kilometres by Eugene Christophe in the 1912 Tour de France. The post-war record is held by Albert Bourlon, who rode the entire 253-kilometre stage from Carcassone to Luchon – including the climbs of the col de Port and the col de Portet d'Aspet – alone from start to finish. *Chapeau* Albert Bourlon!

> **BLUFF IT** ▶ *'You'll always find a good baroudeur in a breakaway'.*

BROOM WAGON/VOITURE BALAI

YOU SAY ► *VWAH – CHEWER BAL*
(as in balance) – EYE

WHAT IS IT? ► They say it ain't over till the fat lady sings. In bike racing it ain't over till the broom wagon goes past, signalling the end of the race. Henri Desgrange introduced the broom wagon in 1910 when the Tour de France first hit the climbs of the high Pyrenees – its purpose was to 'sweep up' riders too ill or exhausted to continue. The original broom wagon was a Citroen H van with an actual broom tied to the back doors. These days, riders are more likely to climb into a team car rather than face the indignity of a ride to the finish line in the *voiture balai*. Whereas in the early days of the Tour, a rider could abandon a stage but still rejoin the race the next day (though his result no longer counted for the overall win) these days an abandon is final and the rider has his race number stripped from his back to prove it. This is the vehicle no rider wants to go home in – French rider Pierrick Fédrigo called his ride in the broom wagon 'a humiliating and humbling experience' and British rider Graham Jones (20th in the 1981 Tour) said of his own experience 'I defy any rider to say that he hasn't shed a tear at climbing into the Tour broom wagon. Maybe not immediately but at some time in that journey to the finish ... the reality will hit home. You climb off the bike followed by the horrible moment when the *commissaire* takes off your race number ... it's an experience that you will never forget.'

BURTON Beryl

BORN ▸ 12 May 1937, Halton (Yorkshire), England
DIED ▸ 8 May 1996, Morley (Yorkshire), England
NATIONALITY ▸ British
RIDER TYPE ▸ Track and road with extraordinary time-trialling capabilities
ACTIVE ▸ 1957–1996
MAJOR ACHIEVEMENTS ▸ 2 × world road race champion (1960, 1967), world pursuit champion (1959, 1960, 1962, 1963, 1966), 13 × national pursuit champion, 12 × national road champion, 18 × national 100-mile time trial champion, 23 × national 50-mile time trial champion, 26 × 25-mile time trial champion, 4 × 10-mile time trial champion (Burton was in her 40s when the 10-mile distance was introduced), British best all-rounder 1959–1983 (25 years!)

Burton was one of Britain's greatest ever athletes, male or female. In terms of sheer number of records she's the female Eddy Merckx, though Marianne Vos *(see V)* is snapping at her heels. Burton shared their competitive spirit too, once refusing to shake hands with her daughter – quite uniquely, mother and daughter both competed for Great Britain – after a race which Denise had won (Beryl claimed it was because she felt her daughter – who had won by the narrowest of margins – 'hadn't done her whack'). Burton was born in Yorkshire, where the Tour de France started in 2014, and held 90 national titles and seven world titles. She held many UK time-trial records and was invited to ride the highly prestigious Grand Prix des Nations – the time trial for elite male riders – in 1967. There was no world championship time trial when Burton was riding, and women's cycling wasn't introduced to the Olympic games until Burton was 47 so how many more rainbow jerseys she might have won or how many gold medals might have hung around her neck remains a tantalising 'what if.' Burton had also set her sights on riding the inaugural women's Tour de France – introduced in the same year as the Olympic women's road race, 1984 – but British Cycling in their wisdom refused, saying she didn't have sufficient road-racing experience. When a rider dropped out at the last minute, Burton was approached to take her place – she none too politely told British Cycling to go and practise a spot of taxidermy on itself ...

But self-financed and with her husband acting as coach, mechanic and *soigneur (see S)*, she was a voracious record setter – the first woman under the hour for 25 miles and she went on to break the two and four-hour barrier for the 50 and 100 miles. A perfectionist, Burton was always trying to better her own records and many stood for 20 years – in fact her 12-hour record of 277.25 miles, set in 1967, still stands, in an age of disc wheels, carbon fibre and skinsuits. Burton died in 1996 at the age of 59, while delivering birthday-party invitations on her bike.

BLUFF FACT ▸ Beryl once rode past a male competitor in a race and offered him a sweet from her jersey pocket – he went on to set a national men's record shorter than the distance Beryl herself set that day. She said later 'the poor dear seemed to be struggling a bit'. His cycling club later honoured her with a huge version of that liquorice allsort.

C IS FOR ...

COPPI Fausto

BORN ▸ 15 September, 1919, Castellania (Piedmont), Italy
DIED ▸ 2 January, 1960, Tortona (Piedmont), Italy
NATIONALITY ▸ Italian
ACTIVE ▸ 1939–1959
RIDER TYPE ▸ All-rounder – Coppi was a superb climber and time triallist
NICKNAME ▸ *Il Campionissimo* (the Champion)
BIG WINS ▸ 5 × Giro d'Italia (1940, 1947, 1949, 1952, 1953), 2 × Tour de France (1949, 1952), 2 × Giro/Tour double (1949, 1952), world champion (1953), 3 × Milan–San Remo (1946, 1948, 1949), 5 × Tour of Lombardy (1946, 1947, 1948, 1949, 1954)
MAJOR RIVAL ▸ Gino Bartali

It's arguable that *il Campionissimo* Fausto Coppi, and not Eddy Merckx, was the greatest rider of all time. He was the first rider to achieve the Giro d'Italia/Tour de France double, and unlike modern riders who tend to specialise in one type of event, Coppi rode all season long and won Grand Tours and Classics in his career. A prisoner of war in the Second World War, what he might have achieved had his career not been interrupted is one of the great 'what ifs' of the sport. He was prone to illness and injury – childhood malnutrition left him with brittle bones and he suffered over 20 major fractures during his career. Coppi was the first man to win on Alpe d'Huez and Puy de Dome in France and the Stelvio in the Italian Alps. Known as 'perfection on two wheels' for his style on the bike, his exploits are both legendary and legion: winning the 1946 Milan–San Remo Classic by 14 minutes, having attacked just five kilometres into the 292-kilometre race; the 1942 hour record

CONTINUED OVERLEAF ▸

that stood for 14 years; the 190 kilometres he rode alone through the high peaks of the Alps in the 1949 Giro, much of it on dirt roads, over the passes of the Colle della Maddalena, Vars, Izoard, Monginevro and, finally, Sestriere before arriving in Pinerolo 11 minutes and 42 seconds ahead of his deadly rival Gino Bartali.

Coppi was dogged with scandal and tragedy during his life – he left his wife for the 'Woman in White', Giulia Occhini, who was married to an army captain. The affair had started in 1948 when the two met at the Tre Valli Varesine race but was made public in 1954 when La Stampa published a photograph of the Italian champion embracing the mysterious woman in a white dress at the finish line of a race in St Moritz. He fathered an illegitimate son, Faustino, incurring the wrath of the Roman Catholic Church who threatened to ex-communicate him – adultery was still frowned upon, even in a modernising Italy and the Pope refused to bless the Giro when Coppi competed. Occhini was forced to have her baby son in Argentina and the couple's hotel room was raided by police eager to see if they were sharing a bed. Coppi had already endured the tragedy of his beloved brother Serse's death. Also a

professional, the younger brother died after injuries sustained in a crash in a race in 1951 where the two brothers had been competing together. Suffering an undiagnosed concussion, Serse died in Fausto's arms.

Coppi arguably invented the modern approach to bike racing – he was meticulous about his diet and training regime, though he was equally open about his use of amphetamines, which he referred to as *la Bomba*. His rivalry with Bartali lit up the roads of Europe but also reflected a wider conflict in Italian society between the religious and the secular, the traditional and the modern. Coppi lived fast and died young – he contracted malaria while racing in Africa and was dead at 40.

When a reporter once asked him what it took to be a great champion, Coppi's answer was simple: 'Ride your bike, ride your bike, ride your bike.'

BLUFF IT ▶ *'Imagine, Coppi's prize for winning his first race aged 15 was 20 lire (about £8) and a salami sandwich'.*

CADENCE

The number of revolutions of the crank per minute (rpm) – in other words, how fast or slow a cyclist is pedalling. The biggest contrast in recent years was between Jan Ullrich – who favoured a big gear and a low cadence (65–70 rpm) – and Lance Armstrong who used smaller gears and rode at 110 rpm. High cadence riding is generally accepted to be better for

overall performance, which Armstrong's success would indicate if he hadn't confessed to doping in 2013.

BLUFF IT ▶ *'Look at rider x twiddling those tiny gears with a high cadence' or conversely 'Look at rider y grinding out those big gears with his low cadence'.*

CARAVAN

They say you've never seen the caravan until you've wrestled a pensioner for a freebie. The caravan is the long string of publicity vehicles that precede the Tour de France – you might catch a keyring, grab a cap or get squirted by the water cannon. You can feed yourself for the day on little sausages (if you like little sausages). All the major sponsors of the Tour have vehicles in the caravan – you'll see the PMU horses, the Festina watches and the Coca Cola wagons. There have been some weird and wonderful vehicles over the years featuring everything from garden gnomes to baguettes. It made a star of Yvette Horner, a young French accordion player, in the 1950s and 60s when she would serenade spectators and podium presentations alike from her specially adapted van. The organisers of the Tour de France say that over 50 per cent of people who watch the race have actually come to see the caravan.

BLUFF IT ▸ *'Did you know there are 160 vehicles in the caravan which give away 16 million items during the three weeks of the race? That's about 32 tons of freebies or the weight of seven elephants.'*

CHAPEAU

YOU SAY ▸ *SHAP (rhymes with nap) – OH (rhymes with low)*

WHAT IT MEANS ▸ A Frenchman's *chapeau* is his hat, and he tips it to indicate a job well done. Love it or loathe it – and many British fans prefer the more Anglocentric 'hat' (or Scottish 'bunnet') – it is the universal term of approval that indicates a good win or a great exploit. So *chapeau* for buying this book!

CHASSE PATATE

YOU SAY ▸ *SHASS (rhymes with lass) PAT – AT*

WHAT IT MEANS ▸ Literally? Hunting potatoes. In a bike race, when a rider is wedged between the breakaway and the peloton, pedalling furiously but making little headway to catch the group ahead, he is *en chasse patate*. It's a term from the old *Vélodrome d'Hiver* (the winter velodrome) in Paris and the six-day races that took place on the boards there. These marathon events, originating in the UK, involved riders refuelling on the go – the sprints to catch the leaders were noticeably slower after dinner whilst the riders digested the contents of their *musettes (see M)*. These slow-motion sprints became known as *chasse-patate*, sometimes translated as ' ploughing potatoes'.

CHEATING

Cycling has become synonymous with doping in recent years, but other forms of cheating have dogged racing over the years. Taking the train, getting a lift in a team car, the 'magic spanner' *(see M)* and the 'sticky bottle' *(see S)* have all helped riders to get to the finish over the years. Riders now get fined for hanging on to the team car too long or accepting a push from a fan.

BLUFF IT ▸ *'In 1904, Hippolyte Aucouturier held a cork between his teeth attached to a piece of wire to get a tow from his team car – hope he had a good dentist.'*

CHUTE

YOU SAY ▶ *SHOOT*

WHAT IT MEANS ▶ Now say 'ow'. Hope you were wearing a helmet – you just learned the French word for crash.

Anything can cause a crash – a narrow pinch point in the road, the fight for position as the peloton head towards a tough section of the race or a stray spectator wanting a closer look at the action – one memorable crash at a Tour de France stage finish in 1994 was caused by a policeman stepping out into the road to take a photo. If you're going to crash in a race, make sure you do it inside the last three kilometres, then you'll be given the same time as the rest of the peloton.

CLASSIC

WHAT IS IT? ▶ A one-day race that's been staged for a number of years is known as a 'Classic'. There are Classic races in the spring and the autumn raced over the flat (Paris–Tours: the Sprinters' Classic), small to medium climbs (Amstel Gold, Flèche Wallonne, Liège –Bastogne–Liège) and, most famously, the cobbles of the Tour of Flanders and Paris–Roubaix. Five of these super-hard races are known as 'the Monuments': Milan–San Remo *(see M)*, Tour of Flanders *(see T)*, Paris–Roubaix *(see P)*, Liège–Bastogne–Liège *(see L)* and the Tour of Lombardy *(see T)*.

Three men have been the King of the Classics, winning all five Monuments in a season, and all three are Belgian – Roger de Vlaeminck, Rik van Looy and of course Eddy Merckx.

> **BLUFF IT** ▶ *'The original Classics could be over 400 kilometres long – the longest is now Milan–San Remo at 298 kilometres or 185 miles – that's like riding from London to Sheffield.'*

CLIMBING

This is part of the key skill set for any jersey contender in a Grand Tour or one of the hilly Classics like Milan–San Remo. Of the great stage-race riders, all have been able to climb with the true mountain goats (think Merckx and Coppi) or been able to stamp their authority on the race in the time trial and then control the climbers in the mountains – that's how Wiggins won the 2012 Tour. But even sprinters need to have some climbing chops if they want to win the points jersey in a Grand Tour.

> **BLUFF IT** ▶ *'You don't wear green in Paris if you can't get over the mountains.'*

COBBLES

See P for Pavé. Britain does have its very own equivalent of the *pavé* climbs of the Tour of Flanders – the Michaelgate in Lincoln is a narrow, cobbled climb with an average 16 per cent gradient, making it the equivalent of the Cauberg.

COMMISSAIRE

YOU SAY ▶ *COM – EE – SAIR (rhymes with hair)*

WHAT IT MEANS ▶ The *commissaire* is cycling's equivalent of an umpire or a referee. It's their job to check a rider's eligibility to compete, to ensure that they're using equipment that complies with the rules and to resolve disputes and judge results. It's the *commissaires* who make the call on a photo finish or declassify a rider for dangerous riding.

CONTADOR Alberto

BORN ▸ 6 December, 1982, Pinto (Madrid), Spain
NATIONALITY ▸ Spanish
ACTIVE ▸ 2003–
RIDER TYPE ▸ All-rounder, climbing specialist
NICKNAME ▸ El Pistolero (Contador has a trademarked finger-bang victory salute)
BIG WINS ▸ 2 × Tour de France (2007, 2009), Giro d'Italia (2008), 2 × Vuelta a España (2008, 2012), 2 × Paris–Nice (2007, 2010)
MAJOR RIVAL ▸ Lance Armstrong, Andy Schleck, Chris Froome

Spain's Alberto Contador is the only Spanish rider to have won all three Grand Tours – the Tour de France, the Giro d'Italia and the Vuelta a España. He has also achieved a rare Giro/Vuelta double in 2008 after his Astana team were not selected for the Tour de France because of the previous year's doping scandals, though the Spaniard was not a member of the team in 2007.

Always an athletic and sporty kid, Contador switched focus from football and athletics to cycling at the age of fourteen when his older brother, Javier (now his manager), introduced him to the sport. The pair had a loving but hardscrabble childhood in Pinto – where Contador continues to live – as their parents struggled to provide for a younger brother with cerebral palsy. Cycling gave the young man an opportunity to help out financially.

Success was swift: he won five Grand Tours in three years, including three Tours de France, though he lost his 2010 victory after failing a test for clenbuterol, which the rider blamed on eating contaminated steak. The race was notable for the infamous 'chaingate' incident on stage 15 when Contador appeared to attack his closest rival, Andy Schleck, after the Luxembourg rider had a mechanical *(see M)* when his chain came off. The incident was controversial because Schleck was wearing the leader's yellow jersey at the time and one of the

COOKE Nicole

BORN ▸ 13 April, 1983, Swansea, Wales
NATIONALITY ▸ Welsh
ACTIVE ▸ 2002–2012
RIDER TYPE ▸ Road and track
NICKNAMES ▸ The Wick Wonder, Cookie
BIG WINS ▸ World champion road race (2008), Olympic road race (2008), Commonwealth Games road race (2002), Women's Giro d'Italia (2004), Women's Tour de France (2006, 2007), 3 × Flèche Wallonne (2003, 2005, 2006), Amstel Gold (2003), Tour of Flanders (2007), 10 × GB national champion
MAJOR RIVAL ▸ Marianne Vos

Nicole Cooke is one of the greatest cyclists the UK has ever produced and one of the best female riders of all time. She began cycling aged 11 and was awarded the Birdlake Memorial Prize for outstanding contribution to British cycling by becoming world mountain bike, road and time-trial champion. But arguably her greatest contribution was her ongoing

sport's unwritten rules is that you don't attack the yellow jersey when he's in trouble – a rule that is oft quoted and rarely observed. Contador took the jersey and held it to the finish line in Paris, only to lose it again when the UCI banned him for two years (the ban was backdated) in 2012.

After winning the 2008 Giro d'Italia with virtually no preparation it was his 2009 Tour win that sealed Contador's reputation as the greatest stage-race talent of his generation. It was a titanic struggle with team-mate Lance Armstrong – Contador would later say he'd had to contest two races, one on the road and one in the hotel, calling the race 'psychologically tough'. Isolated in the team, with Armstrong commandeering not only the best equipment but also the team's entire fleet of cars so the Spaniard was forced to rely on his brother to get back to the team hotel after summit finishes, Contador disobeyed team orders and attacked on the uphill finish to Arcalis in the Pyrenees and finally took the yellow jersey on stage 15, cementing the lead with a victory on the

final time trial in Annecy.

But it might all have been so different – in 2004, Contador collapsed during a race and was rushed to hospital suffering from a cerebral cavernoma (a cluster of abnormal blood cells in the brain), a congenital condition that required delicate surgery and threatened to end his career. The Spaniard maintains that the best victory of his career was winning the queen stage *(see Q)* of the 2008 Tour Down Under in Australia.

BLUFF FACT ▶ Though he was inspired to get into cycling by his compatriot Miguel Indurain, his boyhood heroes were Italian Marco Pantani and America's Lance Armstrong. He claims he read Armstrong's book 'It's Not about the Bike' twice when he was recuperating from his cerebral cavernoma.

BLUFF FACT ▶ 'Contador's first set of cycling gear was homemade. His mum sewed some old shoulder pads into a pair of shorts and cut the toes off some old socks for arm warmers.'

fight to establish British championship racing for girls which has paved the way for a whole generation of stars like Victoria Pendleton and Laura Trott.

Cooke published her autobiography *The Breakaway* in 2014 and continues to campaign for women's cycling.

> **BLUFF IT** ▶ *'Nicole is one of the few cyclists, male or female, to win Olympic gold and the rainbow stripes in the same year'.*

D IS FOR ...

DOMESTIQUE

YOU SAY ▶ *DOM – ES (like the letter S) – TEEK*

WHAT IT MEANS ▶ The literal translation from the French is 'servant', and without the *domestique* there would be no professional cycling as we know it. Their sole job is to help their team leader with no thought of individual glory, because the *domestique* is a strange beast. Though a team of riders start the race, only one has a realistic chance of winning overall glory. The rest may be offered the opportunity of a stage win as recompense for their hard work – or if their team has no realistic chance to take the overall win. And that's the lot of the *domestiques* – to subsume themselves to their leader, the race, the road, to put their nose in the wind so their leader doesn't have to, to give him their bike if his is no longer fit for purpose, to help him climb the heights and descend the other side in safety, to protect and cosset him like so many love-sick drones clustered around their queen bee. The term comes straight from the pen of Henri Desgrange, the man who started the Tour de France, who so hated collusion and collaboration and so prized individual effort that he coined the term for a French rider, Maurice Brocco, when he heard that Brocco had offered his services to another rider to act as a pacemaker. Desgrange was so incensed he described him as 'little better than a *domestique* (servant)', and the term stuck.

DÉPART

YOU SAY ▶ *DAY – PAR*

However you say it, it means the same thing in French and English – the *départ* is the start line of a race. Actually, there are two *départs*, the *départ fictif* and *départ réel*. The *fictif* (literally fictional or false) start of the race is also known as the neutral zone, allowing the peloton to roll slowly out of the start town without any mishaps (though crashes do happen) and the crowds to get a good look at their favourite riders. The *réel* (real) start of the race happens when the race director drops his flag and the racing begins in earnest.

DERAILLEUR

YOU SAY ▶ *The French say DAY – RYE – UR (to rhyme with fur) but in English we usually say DE (as in demand) – RAILER (rhymes with trailer)*
WHAT IT IS ▶ Put *really* simply, the derailleur is a mechanised system that allows you to change gears either on the chainrings (front derailleur) or the cassette (rear derailleur) by clicking on a lever which precisely guides the chain from one chainring or cog to another.

Though various early derailleur mechanisms had been designed in the late 1800s at the height of the bicycle boom, the first recognisable two speed rear derailleur was invented in 1905 and the first raceworthy system appeared in 1928 when Oscar Egg, a Swiss track rider, introduced the 'super champion gear.' But it took another nine years for the derailleur to make its debut at the Tour de France, and even then many riders distrusted the derailleur, considering it unreliable, preferring to use multiple gear ratios instead – because of course dismounting, releasing the chain tension, manually placing the chain on the new cog, repositioning the rear wheel and retensioning the chain was so much easier than using a shifting mechanism to do the work for you. And woe betide if you forgot to tighten your wing nuts ... In 1938 Simplex introduced a cable-shifted derailleur and then, in 1949, the Italian company Campagnolo introduced what is recognised as the first modern derailleur, the Gran Sport.

The effect of the derailleur on the development of modern cycle racing is incalculable – the average speed of the Tour de France jumped sharply and it's said that the *lanterne rouge* or last rider to finish *(see L)* in the 1937 Tour averaged the same speed as

CONTINUED OVERLEAF ▶

the winner of the 1936 Tour. The derailleur impacted on race tactics too – the previous system meant that picking the exact right moment to perform a gear change could be crucial and costly in terms of time and position, particularly on a mountain stage. With the new gear shifting mechanisms that was no longer the case – the ability to change gears simply and easily was literally at a rider's fingertips.

DESGRANGE Henri

'The Father of the Tour', Henri Desgrange was born in Paris in 1865 and was a successful track cyclist setting a dozen world records before he retired and ended up at *l'Auto* where he and Géo Lefèvre were responsible for setting up the Tour de France and single-handedly inventing a brand new sport – bicycle stage racing.

The birth of the Tour de France was a murky one, based as it was on an attempt to destroy a rival newspaper *le Vélo* who had supported Alfred Dreyfus, a French Jew accused of selling secrets to the Germans. *L'Auto* was staunchly anti-Dreyfus – there was more than an unpleasant whiff of antisemitism about the whole Dreyfus Affair. Announced on 19 January, 1903, the first Tour de France was a resounding flop. No one was interested in riding a six-week race round the back roads of France and the expense it would incur. Lefèvre and Desgranges went back to the drawing board, cutting the race to three weeks. Seventy-eight riders signed up, the Tour de France was born and the waning circulation of *l'Auto* more than doubled.

A lifelong cyclist, Desgrange wrote a treatise on cycling *La Tête et les Jambes* ('The Head and the Legs') in 1894, which collected his thoughts on professional bike racing. Among other invaluable pearls of wisdom, Desgrange concluded that a woman was as much use to a cyclist as a dirty pair of socks. But his advice on training and nutrition and his insistence that cycling was as much mental as physical still ring true today. Autocratic and didactic, he viewed the Tour de France as 'the greatest scientific experiment that the sport of cycling has ever given us' and was endlessly meddling with the rules in a doomed attempt to stop riders from collaborating with each other. He is famously supposed to have said: '*Le Tour idéal serait un Tour où un seul coureur réussirait à terminer l'épreuve*' (The ideal Tour would be a Tour where only one rider succeeds in finishing the race). He also pooh-poohed the very idea of new technology, like the derailleur *(see D)*: 'I still feel that variable gears are only for people over 45. Isn't it better to triumph by the strength of your muscles than by the artifice of a derailleur? We are getting soft ... As for me, give me a fixed gear!'

In his fifties, Desgrange went to war in the trenches, serving in the Second World War with the *poilus*, the ordinary soldiers, and winning the *Croix de Guerre* medal for his efforts. Finally ceding control of the race to Jacques Goddet in 1936, he died four years later, leaving as his lasting memorial the greatest cycling race in the world.

BLUFF FACT ► A monument to Henri Desgrange stands at the top of the col du Galibier *(see G)* in the French Alps.

> **BLUFF IT** '*Desgrange was so worried the first Tour de France would be a disaster, he didn't actually turn up to watch it.*'

DEVIL

Didi Senft (retired), better known as Didi the Devil, is a German bicycle designer who has been a fixture at European races since 1993. Clad head to toe in red lycra and brandishing a trident, his horns, luxuriant beard and exuberant roadside antics – including his trademark two footed jump – have won him fans around the world. His trademark trident symbol has appeared on the roads of all the major races, particularly the Tour de France. Didi travels with his creations – which include the largest bike in the world – and features in the Guinness Book of Records as the creator of the world's largest mobile guitar. Alas, a combination of lack of sponsorship and ill health saw Didi hang up his trident in 2014, but he has spawned a host of imitators, including the Specialized Angel and American Horn Guy – and every spectator who has ever chased the peloton in a lime green Borat mankini.

DIRECTEUR SPORTIF

YOU SAY ▸ *DEE – WRECK – TUR (as in turn) SPORT – EEF (rhymes with reef)*
The top dog during any cycle race – the *directeur sportif* is just that – the sports director – the man in the team car who decides the tactics that will be used during the race, and who makes the decisions about which riders will make up the team. He communicates with the team via radio giving out information on hazards, crashes and time gaps. The team car will usually carry a team mechanic and spare bikes, as well as drinks, energy bars and gels, medical equipment and the sticky bottle *(see S)* and magic spanner *(see M)*.
BLUFF FACT ▸ In 2014, Rachel Heal made history by becoming the first woman *directeur sportif* at a men's World Tour race.

DNS/DNF

These abbreviations are often seen in race results and mean 'did not start' and 'did not finish'. Three letters that spell the end of the hopes, dreams and ambitions of any rider who stood on the start line with aspirations of glory.

DOPING

Don't do it. Sadly, professional cycling has never taken this wise advice. From the very earliest days of the sport, there have been accusations of poisoned *bidons* – like the one handed to Paul Duboc in the 1911 Tour de France – and the finger was already being pointed at certain doctors in the 1920 Tour de France when Louis Mottiat was forced to abandon the race after getting into 'the unpleasant habit of riding on drugs'. Then the Pélissier brothers gave an incendiary interview to Albert Londres – the 'father of modern investigative journalism' – in 1924 when they claimed they rode 'on dynamite' and showed Londres the content of their bag of tricks that included cocaine, chloroform and amphetamines. Londres coined the nickname *les forçats de la route* (prisoners of the road) for professional cyclists.

But there were more serious problems to come. In 1955 Jean Malléjac would collapse on Mont Ventoux and expose cycling's dirtiest secrets to a watching world. Race doctor Pierre Dumas battled to save the Frenchman and this time he would be successful, though Malléjac never rode again. Twelve years later, Dumas would not be so lucky when Tom Simpson collapsed and died as a result of a fatal combination of amphetamines and alcohol and heat in 1967 – like an ecstasy death at 2000 metres. The events on

CONTINUED OVERLEAF ▸

Mont Ventoux led Dr Dumas to become involved in the drafting of anti-doping legislation, and in 1966 Herzog's Law saw the first ever doping controls take place at the race, with Raymond Poulidor the first rider ever to be tested at the Tour de France.

Times, and methods of performance enhancement, were changing. When the entire Dutch PDM team withdrew from the 1991 Tour de France suffering from a mysterious illness, it was blamed on badly stored intralipid which was being used as a dietary supplement. In fact the team were using a new product, Erythropoietin (EPO). Naturally produced by the kidneys, EPO stimulates red blood cell production which means more oxygen can be carried to tired muscles that can then keep going for longer. The benefit for athletes was obvious, with an Australian study showing that improvements in performance produced in four weeks could match those normally achieved over several years. In 1998 the entire Festina team was forced to withdraw from the Tour de France after their *soigneur* Willy Voet was stopped at the French border with a cargo of performance enhancing drugs, including EPO. Professional cycling was entering its darkest period, with American Lance Armstrong finally stripped of his record breaking seven wins in 2012 after admitting that he'd used a cocktail of drugs and blood transfusions to achieve his success.

DOSSARD

YOU SAY ► *DOSS (rhymes with boss) – AR (like the letter R)*

WHAT IT MEANS ► This is the race number every rider wears. In the Tour de France the red *dossard* is worn by the most aggressive and attacking rider in the race (often the one who has spent the most time in a breakaway), the winner of the 'most combative rider' award, who used to win his weight in cheese. The leading team in the race wears yellow race numbers.

DOWNHILL

Going downhill is the best part of going uphill. Professional cyclists can reach speeds of 110 km/h (65 mph) on a fast descent, but the world record was achieved by Éric Barone who rode down a mountain (on snow, of course) at a speed of 222 kph (138 mph) in 2000.

DRAFTING

(See also Aerodynamics.) Not to be confused with wheelsucking *(see W)*, drafting allows riders to conserve energy and to recover after taking a turn at the front of the group. Not only can you shelter from the wind behind another rider but you benefit from being carried along in the air pocket they create. The energy saving benefits can be anything from 20 to 40 per cent and help both riders because the following rider helps to reduce the turbulence for the leading rider. The benefits of drafting are huge in races or stages which can last six hours and see riders burning over 10,000 calories.

But stay vigilant – it's easy to become so glued to another rider's wheel that you forget to react to what's going on and that's when chutes can occur *(see C)*.

E IS FOR ...

ÉQUIPE

YOU SAY ► EH – KEEP

WHAT IT MEANS ► A team – in this case a professional cycling team. Each cycling team has its support staff: manager, *directeur sportif (see D)*, *soigneurs (see S)*, mechanics, trainers and medical staff – and riders: sprinters *(see S)*, *rouleurs (see R)*, *puncheurs (see P)* and *grimpeurs*. Some teams, like Team Sky, focus on winning races overall and support a team leader, other teams may focus on stage wins only, or winning one of the other classifications like points, king of the mountains or young rider. The team targets and the type of race are crucial in deciding which riders will make up the team. For Paris–Roubaix *(see P)* you need big, strong *rouleurs* who can go flat out on the cobbles, for the Vuelta a España *(see V)* you'll need a whole raft of climbers for the mountaintop finishes.

EQUIPIER

YOU SAY ► AY-KEEP-EE-AY

Every *equipe* is made up of *equipiers* or teammates who support their team leader for the General Classification *(see G)*. These riders can be sprinters, lead out men, climbers or *rouleurs* – the strong men who can ride kilometere after kilometre at the head of the peloton. Together they combine into a unit designed to deliver their leader to the top step of the podium with little chance of personal glory.

BLUFF IT ► *'Tradition says that the winner of a race divides his prize money with his faithful* equipiers*'*

ECHELON

YOU SAY ► *ESH (to rhyme with mesh) – A – LON*

WHAT IT MEANS ► An echelon is a diagonal formation of riders that happens when the peloton gets hit by a crosswind. Riders seek shelter behind each other, overlapping their front wheel with the rear wheel of the rider in front and fanning out across the road so the lead rider takes the full force of the wind for as long as he can before dropping to the back of the echelon. Crosswinds often cause huge gaps and riders can lose a lot of time and waste a lot of energy if they're not in the front group when the peloton splits.

RIDER

EVANS Cadel

BORN ► 14 February, 1977, Katherine (Northern Territory), Australia

NATIONALITY ► Australian

ACTIVE ► 1999–

RIDER TYPE ► All-rounder, solid in the climbs and time trials

NICKNAME ► Cuddles

BIG WINS ► Tour de France (2011), world road race champion (2009), Tour of Romandie (2006, 2011), Tirreno-Adriatico (2011), Critérium International (2012)

MAJOR RIVALS ► Andy Schleck, Alberto Contador, Bradley Wiggins

Cadel Evans became the first Australian to wear the rainbow jersey of the world road race champion in 2009 with a daring last minute attack and then went on to take the biggest prize of them all, the Tour de France in 2011, the first win by a rider from the Southern Hemisphere.

Evans came to road racing from mountain biking, having made his way up through the Australian Institute of Sport mountain bike programme. Switching to the road full time in 2000, Evans burst on the scene at the 2002 Giro d'Italia where he wore the pink jersey for one day before suffering a meltdown the next day and losing over 17 minutes. The Australian would wear the *maglia rosa* again but not until 2010.

But it was at the Tour that Evans shone brightest, finishing second in 2007 and 2008. Finally, in 2011, at the age of 34, Evans took the yellow jersey to the Champs-Élysées, though the final stage was the only time he'd worn it throughout the race having finished second behind Germany's Tony Martin on the penultimate time-trial stage and having put significant time into Luxembourg's Schleck brothers who finished second and third on the podium.

Evans, who speaks fluent Italian, is married to an Italian music teacher and they are parents to an adopted son, Robel who had been abandoned on the streets of Shashamane, Ethiopia. The Australian is known for his charitable works and is a vocal supporter of the Free Tibet movement, having worn an undershirt emblazoned with the Tibetan flag in 2008, to draw attention to violent unrest in that country.

BLUFF IT ► *'Calling Evans "Cuddles" is a bit of an in-joke – the Australian is notoriously prickly with the media and once told a reporter at the 2008 Tour de France "Don't stand on my dog, or I'll cut your head off!"'*

ÉTAPE

YOU SAY ► *EH – TAP*

WHAT IT MEANS ► A stage of a stage race – these are the mini one-day races that go to make up a short stage race like Paris–Nice or the Tour of California or a three-week Grand Tour. There are five types of stages:

- **Flat stages:** these nearly always end in a sprint finish
- **Rolling stages:** these tend to favour a breakaway
- **Mountain stages:** these are the dramatic stages where the race is decided; the most difficult mountain stage is referred to as the *étape reine* or queen stage
- **Individual time trial:** each rider against the clock, these can often decide the outcome of a race, especially in one-week races, and can be ridden on flat or rolling terrain or up to a mountaintop finish
- **Team time trial:** each team rides against the clock; these usually happen in the first week of a race while teams are still complete

What is generally considered to be the hardest ever stage took place in the 1926 Tour de France. The fearsome 'Circle of Death' – Col d'Ousqich, Col d'Aubisque, Cirque du Litor, Col du Soulor, Col du Tourmalet, Col d'Aspin and Col de Peyresourde (323 kilometres with 6000 metres of climbing on unmade roads) – was ridden in the worst that mother nature could throw at the grim-faced riders. It was Dantesque in its hellishness, with the peloton battling through torrential rain, freezing fog and thunderstorms. The cold was so intense it was virtually impossible to repair a puncture with frozen fingers and icicles formed on faces and bicycle frames. It took the winner, Lucien Buysse, 17 hours and 12 minutes to complete the stage. The last 11 riders over the line took the bus.

EXPLOIT

When a rider goes on a long, lone breakaway *(see B)* or puts in an extraordinary effort to climb a mountain or beat allcomers in a time trial or even struggles to the finish alone simply to stay in the race they are said to have achieved 'a great exploit'. Some good examples of the great exploit are:

Frenchman Albert Bourlon's 1947 stage win in the Tour de France – Bourlon got away at the very start of the 253 km stage and stayed away, alone, crossing the Col de Port and the Col de Portet d'Aspet in the Pyrenees on his way to the finish line. He beat the peloton by sixteen minutes.

Spain's Miguel Indurain rode probably the greatest ever time trial in the Tour de France in 1992. Stage 9 of the race was a 65-kilometre time trial around Luxembourg which Indurain rode at an average speed of more than 45km/h to win in a time of 1 hour 19 minutes and 31 seconds. He caught France's Laurent Fignon who started six minutes ahead of him and beat the next fastest rider by three minutes. Indurain simply steamrollered the rolling hilly course – and that year's Tour de France.

Italy's Claudio Chiappucci honoured the memory of his compatriot Fausto Coppi by replicating *il Campionissimo*'s fabulous ride to Sestriere in the 1952 Tour exactly 40 years later. Where Coppi had attacked and gone clear over the Croix de Fer, the Galibier, Montgenèvre and then won at Sestriere by seven minutes (all the more remarkable because he'd become the first man ever to win on France's Alpe d'Huez the day before), the diminutive Chiappucci – nicknamed the Little Devil – pulled off a different feat that was equally epic. Attacking from the gun, he crossed the climbs of the Col de Saisies (category 2), Cornet de Roseland (category 2), Col d'Iseran (hors catégorie), Mont Cenis (category 1) and the final climb to the finish at Sestriere (category 1) alone to prove his panache was worthy of comparison with his idol. Chiappucci did it in the polka dot jersey of the king of the mountains, Coppi did it in the race leader's yellow jersey.

At six foot four inches, Italy's Eros Poli was the tallest *domestique (see D)* of the 1990s, and in the 1994 Tour de France he pulled off an extraordinary solo ride to cross the top of the fearsome Mont Ventoux *(see V)* then dived down the other side to claim an emotional victory 40 kilometres later. Usually to be found in the autobus *(see A)* in the mountains, this was the day that the big man bested the little mountain climbers and gave MAMILs (middle aged men in lycra) everywhere something to cheer.

In the 1983 Tour de France, Frenchman Pascal Simon took the yellow jersey – and a four minute lead – in the Pyrenees. The very next day he crashed and fractured his shoulder blade. And so began his battle to try and save the yellow jersey. Refusing to abandon the race, he rode on for five more days until he was forced to climb off his bike on the stage to Alpe d'Huez – it was a stage too far even for Simon's bravery and courage. 'I tried to go as far as possible. But I'm too bad,' he said. 'Tonight I'm sad. It's the last time I'll wear the yellow jersey.' Pascal was right, he never wore the jersey again. But there is a twist. In 2001 his brother François, who had grown up envying his brother's framed jerseys on the wall of the family home, was close to taking the yellow jersey for himself. Before the day's stage he had a telephone call from his brother Pascal: 'He told me he'd had to leave the jersey in the Alps and that it was up to me to go and get it for him.' Later that day François pulled on the yellow jersey on Alpe d'Huez, eighteen years after his brother had been forced to abandon it there.

But the real beauty of the exploit is that it's in the eye of the beholder – and part of the fun of watching cycling is noticing those moments when a rider goes above and beyond and pulls off a ride that you remember forever.

F IS FOR ...

FLAMME ROUGE

YOU SAY ▸ *FLAM (rhymes with lamb) ROOZH (the final sound like the 's' in vision)*

WHAT IT MEANS ▸ The *flamme rouge* (literally, red flame) or red kite is the triangular-shaped red pennant that's displayed one kilometre from the finish line. It usually hangs from an inflatable arch over the road. A good spot to stand as a spectator because the *flamme rouge* is always televised. First used in the 1906 Tour de France, maybe Henri Desgrange was thinking of the way armies would use a red flag to show they were going into battle. The *flamme rouge* has certainly been the start of plenty of great sprinting battles over the years.

FALSE FLAT

The point in a climb when the gradient eases off and the climb becomes much easier is known as a false flat. You're still climbing but, in comparison to what's gone before, it feels like you're rolling along a country lane.

FEED ZONE

The French call this the *ravitaillement* which means to restock or replenish. It's the somewhat chaotic moment you see during a race when the helpers from different teams jostle for position in the road to get their *musettes (see M)* to their riders so they can eat during the stage. The feed zone is generally agreed to be a neutral point in the race but some riders do take advantage of the general confusion to launch an attack – which is a quick way to make enemies. Attacking your rivals while they're eating is fair game though – it's how Fabian Cancellara beat Tom Boonen in the 2010 Paris–Roubaix, the Swiss rider taking off as the Belgian enjoyed a snack.

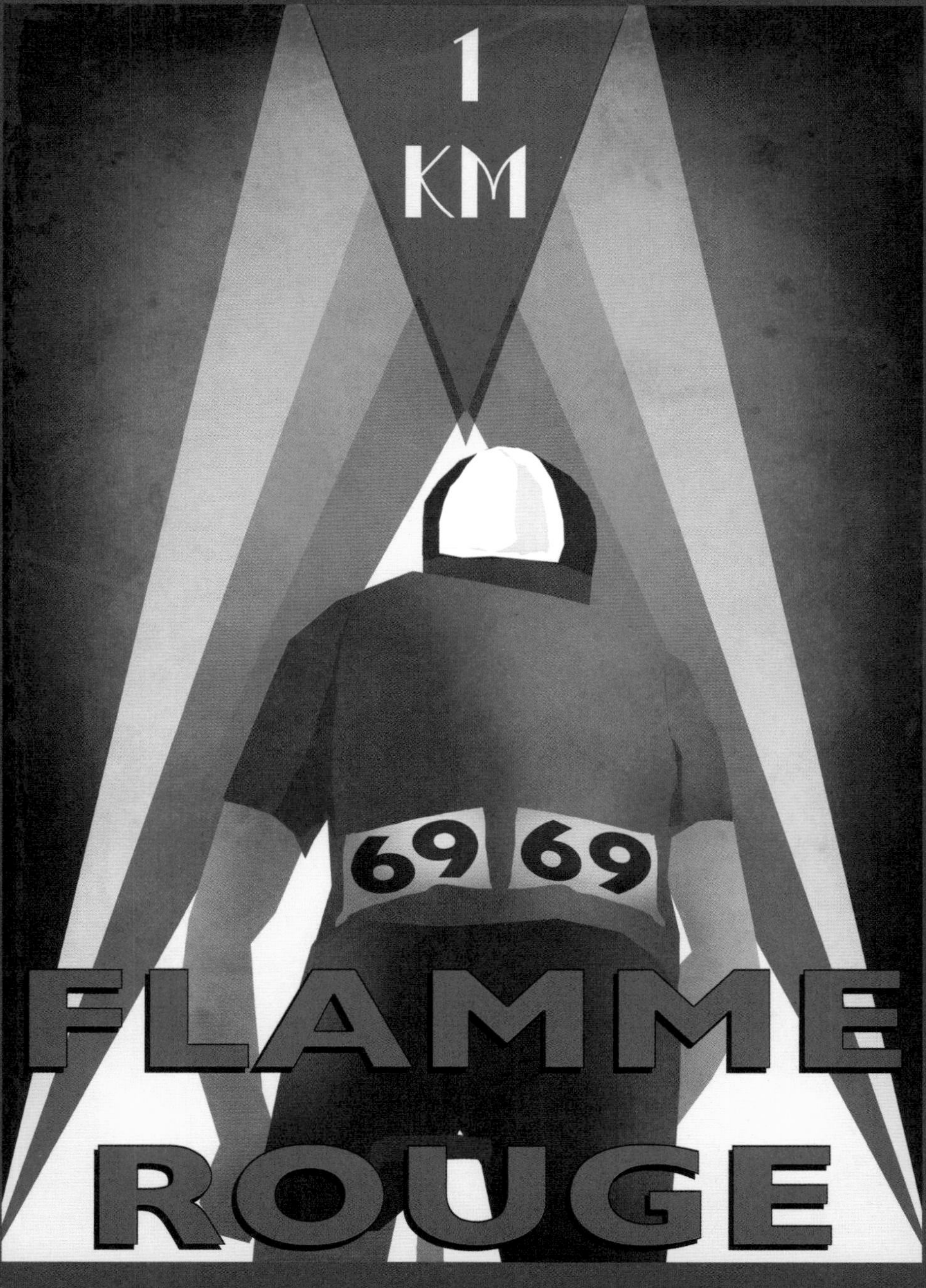
1
KM
69 69
FLAMME
ROUGE

FESTINA AFFAIR

When Willy Voet, a *soigneur (see S)* with the Festina team was stopped by customs officials on 8 July, 1998, and discovered to have a carload of doping products, it set in train a series of events that would impact not just the Tour de France but the sport as a whole, and whose repercussions are still being felt. It was a race within the race that nobody wanted to watch and became known throughout the sport as the Festina Affair.

Voet was charged with 'importation of contraband products and trafficking in forbidden products', and it quickly emerged that he was acting under orders from team management. Bruno Roussel, the team's *directeur sportif (see D)* was arrested and admitted that his riders had been doping under medical supervision, at which point the Festina team were excluded from the race. The immediate impact on the Tour was huge. There were a series of police raids with several teams – the Dutch team TVM, the Italian team Riso Scotti and all of the Spanish teams – withdrawing from the race, reducing the peloton to 96 finishers from the 189 riders who had stood on the start line in Dublin. The riders also staged two sit-down protests on stages 12 and 17 in support of their colleagues who had been subjected to police searches and arrests.

Of the top-ten finishers, only two have not subsequently been linked to any doping scandals. The race winner, Marco Pantani who had become the last rider to achieve the Giro d'Italia/Tour de France double, would retroactively test positive for EPO and died of a cocaine overdose in 2004. All nine riders of the Festina team would eventually admit to taking performance-enhancing drugs during the 1998 Tour.

Did cycling learn its lesson? The 1999 Tour was won by Lance Armstrong – and Festina continue to be the official timekeepers of the Tour de France.

FLAHUTE

YOU SAY ▶ *FLAH (rhymes with baa) – OOT (rhymes with hoot)*

WHAT IT MEANS ▶ The *flahute* is the hardest of the hard men – the tougher the race and the weather conditions, the better these riders like it. As a cycling term it seems to have come into common usage by French journalists after the Second World War, coined as an elaborate joke deriving from the friendly rivalry between the two countries. It derives from the Dutch *flaauwte* meaning failure or weakness and was originally used interchangeably with Flandrian. Once a colloquial term for the angelica plant – a delicate head on a sturdy stem – *flahute* came to designate a strapping young lad, who was a little oblivious or soft in the head. On second thoughts, given the Flahute's love of riding hard in the most miserable of weather, it's bang on the money.

> **BLUFF IT** ▶ '"Mr Paris–Roubaix" Roger de Vlaeminck, the "King of the Classics" Rik Van Looy and "The Boss" Rik Van Steenburgen were three of the great flahutes.'

FLANDERS

The heartland of Belgian cycling, with its well-marked cycle routes, cyclocentric culture and raft of Classic one-day races, Flanders is a cyclist's paradise. The Dutch-speaking northern part of Belgium, Flanders lives and breathes cycling and has produced some of the greatest riders the sport has ever seen and plays host to one of the greatest of the Classics, the Tour of Flanders *(see T)*.

FRINGALE

WHAT IT MEANS ► You know that empty, hollow, exhausted feeling you sometimes get when your blood sugar drops through the floor? Now imagine that experience while riding a bike and you'll have a sense of what a professional cyclist experiences in a race. A *fringale* – or hunger knock or bonking (think Chris Froome on Alpe d'Huez in 2013 rather than Austin Powers) – can leave a cyclist absolutely depleted of energy until they have something to eat or drink. Sometimes known as the 'man with the hammer' for the way it knocks all the force out of your body, a *fringale* on the climb to Les Arcs robbed Miguel Indurain of a record sixth consecutive Tour in 1996 – as the other contenders rode away from him, the Spaniard appeared to be pedalling on the spot unable to follow them. Water, sports drinks, energy gels and power bars are all good ways to deal with a *fringale* as is eating and drinking little and often.

RIDER

FROOME CHRISTOPHER

BORN ► 20 May, 1985, Nairobi, Kenya
NATIONALITY ► British
RIDER TYPE ► All-rounder, with strong time-trialling and climbing abilities
ACTIVE ► 2007–
NICKNAMES ► Froomedog, Froomey
BIG WINS ► Tour de France (2013), Critérium du Dauphiné (2013), Tour de Romandie (2013, 2014), Critérium International (2013)
MAJOR RIVALS ► Bradley Wiggins, Nairo Quintana, Alberto Contador

Chris Froome is the first rider born on the African continent to win the Tour de France, though he currently holds a British racing licence as his father and grandparents were born in Britain. Froome is as capable of beating the best in the world in a time trial as he is of dominating in the mountains. Although he turned professional at the age of 22, it wasn't until his second place at the Vuelta in 2011 that the world of professional cycling began to sit up and take notice of the tall, slight cyclist from Kenya. Overcoming asthma and the tropical parasitic disease bilharzia to become the best in the world, Froome credits David Kinjah, arguably Kenya's only elite cyclist, as mentoring him to glory.

The Briton has been at the heart of one of cycling's favourite soap opera plots – the inter-team rivalry between himself and Bradley Wiggins, which boiled over at the finish of stage 11 of the 2012 race, on the climb to La Toussuire. Clearly the stronger climber of the two, Froome appeared to attack his team leader – and holder of the yellow jersey – Sir Bradley Wiggins *(see W)*, four kilometres from the stage finish. The incident was dismissed as a 'misunderstanding' but it later emerged that Wiggins had threatened to leave the race and refused to pay Froome his share of a £1 million bonus (though Froome did receive his share of the

Tour de France prize money – the winner traditionally splits the winner's purse with his team and support staff for helping him to the victory).

But with undisputed team leadership in the 2013 race, after Wiggins suffered a knee injury before the Tour, Froome was simply untouchable. He won three stages including the mountaintop finish on Mont Ventoux where he launched an extraordinary attack that left his rivals standing with only Colombia's Nairo Quintana *(see Q)* capable of staying anywhere near the Briton in the mountains. When Froome rode up the Champs-Élysées as the winner of the hundredth Tour de France, it was the end of a journey that had started with a mountain bike on the dusty roads of Africa.

BLUFF IT ► *'Froomey's favourite hobby is spear fishing.'*

G IS FOR ...

GIRO D'ITALIA

WHERE ▸ Italy

TYPE OF RACE ▸ Stage race (three weeks), 21 stages with two rest days

STAGES ▸ Flat (sprints), mixed (breakaway), mountains (climbing specialists), time trial (specialists against the clock)

TIME OF YEAR ▸ May–June

MULTIPLE WINS ▸ Alfredo Binda (Italy), Fausto Coppi (Italy) and Eddy Merckx (Belgium) have all won the Giro five times.

MOST WINS BY COUNTRY ▸ Not surprisingly, Italy

GREAT MOMENTS ▸ Fausto Coppi dominating the 1949 Giro before he became the first man to do the Giro-Tour double; Andy Hampsten pulling on the pink jersey after crossing the Gavia in a blizzard in 1988; Pantani recovering from a mechanical to pass 49 riders and win on the climb to Oropa; Nairo Quintana becoming the first ever Colombian winner of a Grand Tour in 2014.

JERSEYS ▸ Leader's jersey: pink (*maglia rosa*); sprint jersey: red; mountains jersey: blue; young rider: white

The second oldest of the Grand Tours, the Giro d'Italia dates from 1909. Like the Tour de France, it was organised by a newspaper, the *Gazzetta dello Sport,* who modelled the Giro on a car race run by rival Italian newspaper *Corriere della Sera,* and like the Tour has a leader's jersey in the colour of the paper's pages, in this case pink. Still a more intimate race than the Tour, it wasn't won by a non-Italian until 1950 and continues to be dominated by riders from the Boot. Where the roads of France are lined with holidaymakers out to enjoy the carnival atmosphere and watch the caravan pass

CONTINUED OVERLEAF ▸

by, the roads of Italy are lined with the *tifosi (see T)*, the fiercely passionate and knowledgeable fans who often cycle to the roadside to see their heroes go past.

For the history of the Giro is dominated by its great champions or '*campioni*', the heroic riders who stamped their personality and authority on the race. Its history is entwined with that of Coppi and Bartali, Magni and Binda, who won the race five times in the 20s and 30s and held the record for most stage wins in the Giro until the Italian sprinter Mario Cipollini broke it in 2003. It's a measure of how important the race is to the Italian riders that when, in 1956, Magni broke his collarbone in a crash during a hellish descent he rode on, controlling his bike with an inner tube doubled round the handlebars and gripped in his teeth. He finished second behind the great climber Charly Gaul.

But it's in its topography that Italy really puts one over on its French cousin, allowing the Giro to enjoy a much more challenging route with far more difficult climbs than the French race. The gradients are steeper and more demanding than anything to be found in the French Alps or Pyrenees. Brutal, sadistic, terrible – this is how the greatest riders in the history of the sport have described the Giro. But none have been able to resist its allure, and for the *tifosi* you're not a real champion until you've conquered the roads of Italy.

> **BLUFF IT ▸** *'It's the toughest race in the world's most beautiful place.' (This is how race organisers RCS describe the Giro.)*

CLIMB

GALIBIER

YOU SAY ▸ *GAH (rhymes with ha!) – LEE – BEE – AY (rhymes with hay)*

ALTITUDE ▸ 2645 metres
HEIGHT GAIN ▸ 1216 metres
AVERAGE GRADIENT ▸ 7 per cent
MAXIMUM GRADIENT ▸ 10 per cent
LENGTH ▸ 18 kilometres
LOCATION ▸ French Alps

The Galibier isn't the highest pass in the Alps, but it's often the highest pass in the Tour and as such regularly sees the first rider over the top awarded the 'souvenir Henri Desgrange'. This is the pass where Desgrange has his memorial, and a wreath is always laid when the Tour passes. The first fatality in the Tour de France occurred when 29-year-old Francisco Cepeda plunged into a ravine on the descent of the Galibier in 1935 and died on his way to hospital, his skull fractured, without regaining consciousness. It was the springboard for Fausto Coppi's leap into greatness when he attacked on the Galibier in the 1952 Tour de France and soloed his way into Italy and a famous win at Sestriere. Marco Pantani sealed his 1998 Tour de France victory when he took off on the Galibier en route to a win at Les Deux Alps which crushed the hopes of Jan Ullrich. When Andy Schleck won there in the 2011 Tour de France he rode for 60 kilometres alone across the Izoard to finish on the mighty heights of what Henri Desgrange called 'the giant'.

GAVIA

YOU SAY ▸ *GAH – VEE – AH*
ALTITUDE ▸ 2621 metres
HEIGHT GAIN ▸ 1363 metres
AVERAGE GRADIENT ▸ 7.9 per cent
MAXIMUM GRADIENT ▸ 16 per cent
LENGTH ▸ 17.3 kilometres
LOCATION ▸ Italian Alps

One man is linked above all others with the fearsome Gavia pass. If you Google 'Gavia Pass' you will see an image of him, battling through a snowstorm. That man is Andy Hampsten and his ride over the Gavia on stage 14 in the 1988 Giro d'Italia is the stuff of legend – they call it 'the day the hard men cried'. On the toughest stage in modern bike racing, the American ascended the narrow track that carves its way up the Gavia, past the ominous markers to those who have plunged to their deaths, up the endless hairpins with the gradient that ramps up relentlessly, through a blizzard that had dumped more than a metre of snow on the Gavia pass overnight and that continued to fall in thick, fat flurries, soaking the riders to the skin and freezing them to their core. Hampsten's team had prepared by smearing themselves in lanolin, the grease that cross-channel swimmers use to combat the incessant cold, and he wore heavy, cumbersome neoprene gloves. Stalactites of ice hung from riders' faces and handlebars as the temperature at the summit of the 2621-metre monster plummeted. Hampsten had attacked on one of the narrowest and hardest sections of the climb and continued to pour on the pressure, ploughing on through the snowstorm as the rest of the peloton exploded behind him. On the descent, into a shaded valley where the sun never penetrates even on a warm day, conditions worsened as the riders plummeted into the teeth of the storm. Riders were peeing on their hands to force some feeling back into their frozen fingers. Others were huddled in their team cars drinking hot tea laced with brandy. The hardest men of a hard sport stood by the side of the road and cried with the pain and the effort of battling the appalling conditions. Hampsten didn't win the stage that day – a Dutch rider Erik Breukink passed him six kilometres from the finish line and the American was unable to respond – but he did ride himself into history when he stood on the podium and took the pink jersey, the only American ever to win the Giro d'Italia.

GENERAL CLASSIFICATION

The *classement général* is the classification that decides the overall winner of a stage race. It works like this: the time each rider records on each stage is added together and the rider who takes the least time wins. Of course there are some sleights of hand involved – in a sprint finish, every rider finishing in the bunch is given the same time – unless there's a split of more than one second, in which case those riders are given their individual time when they cross the line. In the general classification, every second counts.

RIDER

GIMONDI Felice

BORN ▶ 29 September, 1942, Sedrina (Bergamo), Italy
NATIONALITY ▶ Italian
ACTIVE ▶ 1965–1978
RIDER TYPE ▶ All-rounder
NICKNAME ▶ The Phoenix
BIG WINS ▶ Tour de France (1965), 3 × Giro d'Italia (1967, 1969, 1976), Vuelta a España (1968), world road race champion (1973), Milan–San Remo (1974), Paris–Roubaix (1966), 2 × Giro di Lombardia (1966, 1973)
MAJOR RIVAL ▶ Eddy Merckx

Felice Gimondi would have a stellar career by any standards with 158 career victories, the only Italian rider to date to win all three Grand Tours and the only rider besides Merckx and Hinault to have won the five greatest races in the sport: the three Grand Tours, Paris–Roubaix and the world championships. But when you consider that he was riding mainly in the era of the Cannibal, Eddy Merckx, his achievements are that little bit more remarkable, and the 'what ifs' more poignant. He said of his adversary, 'I always felt like I was bashing my head against a brick wall.'

Gimondi was a complete champion and he showed every ounce of his skills in his first ever Tour de France in 1965 sealing a memorable win with victory in the final stage, a flat TT from Versailles to Paris. It was all the more extraordinary because Gimondi hadn't wanted to race the Tour de France at all – he thought it was too hard and, at 22, his *directeur sportif* felt he was too young. He was a last minute replacement for another rider and when he was invited to the race he replied, 'Wait,

I'll just ask my dad.' Finding out he'd be riding the race on the Thursday evening before it started, he had just enough time to get from Furli to his home in Sedrina, pack a bag and head for the start line in Cologne. His *directeur sportif*, Luciano Pezzi, his eyes full of tears said, 'On the road from Versailles to Paris, I believed I was watching Coppi.'

Gimondi had arrived on the scene in 1964 by winning the Tour de l'Avenir (The Race of the Future), the proving ground for future champions. And Gimondi was the best in the world, the new *Campionissimo* through the 1960s until the arrival of Merckx. He bookended his career with Grand Tour wins, taking the 1976 Giro at the age of 34. An outsider, he beat the great Belgian on a stage into Bergamo – he had also beaten Merckx to become world champion in 1973 – then took the time trial the following day and pulled on the pink jersey for one last great win. But despite being rivals, the two have maintained a friendship and respect in their personal lives with Merckx calling him 'the epitome of dignity' and openly admiring his courtesy and strength of character.

Gimondi retired from racing on a wet and miserable day in 1978. Riding the Giro dell'Emilia with his old friend Franco Bitosi, lacking in motivation and at the back end of a superb career, the two men looked at each other and decided: 'We don't want to get wet again, let's stop here'. It was the end of the road for the last great Italian champion.

GIRO DI LOMBARDIA

WHERE ► Italy

TYPE OF RACE ► One-day Classic

TAKES PLACE IN ► Lombardy, in Italy

NICKNAME ► The Race of the Falling Leaves

TERRAIN ► Undulating, medium mountains

TIME OF YEAR ► Autumn

MULTIPLE WINS ► Fausto Coppi (5 wins)

MOST WINS BY COUNTRY ► Italy

GREAT MOMENTS ► Fiorenzo Magni riding almost 60 kilometres in pursuit of Fausto Coppi and catching him as the race entered Milan because he felt Coppi's mistress had sneered at him – both were beaten by a Frenchman, André Darrigade, in the sprint; Herman

CONTINUED OVERLEAF ►

Van Springel winning solo in 1968 and beating Jan Janssen who had beaten him in the Tour de France by 38 seconds; Paolo Bettini winning solo in the world champions jersey in 2006, days after his brother was killed in a car accident – the Italian crossed the line in tears.

Though the Giro di Lombardia has been in existence since 1905, when it was called Milan–Milan, it wasn't until 1961 that, with a single stroke of genius, the modern race was born. Instead of facing a long, flat run in back to Milan, race organisers decided that the race would finish in Como, on the shores of the beautiful lake, with the finish line just 6 kilometres from the final climb. The last Classic of the season, the race is one of the most beautiful as it weaves its way through avenues of golden Lombardy poplars around the majestic shores of Lake Como.

The Giro di Lombardia is characterised by a series of short, sharp climbs, with none more iconic than the climb from the shores of the lake to the chapel of Madonna di Ghisallo, a shrine to the great riders who have graced the roads of Italy and beyond. It is the only cycling museum to be blessed by a pope. Every year when the race climbs the 10 kilometres to her chapel, the bells are rung to greet the riders.

BLUFF IT ▸ *'The Madonna di Ghisallo was named the patron saint of cyclists in 1949.'*

GRADIENT

The simplest way to work out the gradient of a climb is dividing the 'rise' of the climb (its height) by the 'run' (the length of the climb):

GRADIENT = RISE ÷ RUN × 100

Most of us prefer to do our cycling on a 0 per cent gradient, that is, on a flat, level road. 1–3 per cent will have you working a little harder – imagine riding into a stiff headwind. 4–6 per cent and you'll start to feel it in your legs, especially if it's over a long distance. 7–9 per cent and you're approaching the kind of gradients that professional cyclists take in their stride on a lumpy stage but which would put many everyday cyclist on their knees. 10–15 per cent and you're on a *hors catégorie (see H)* climb, hanging on to the autobus *(see A)* if you're lucky. Anything above that and, unless you're a highly trained professional cyclist, you'll most likely get off and walk. Strength, fitness and gearing are all crucial in coping with even the slightest gradients.

GRAND TOUR

The three Grand Tours of cycling are the Tour de France (1903), the Giro d'Italia (1909) and the Vuelta a España (1935). They are the only races allowed to extend beyond 14 days and follow a strict format laid down by the UCI *(see U)*. No longer do cyclists have to ride through the night to complete marathon stages of more than 300 kilometres – stages cannot exceed 240 kilometres and the maximum daily average must not exceed 180 kilometres. Time trials can be no longer than 60 kilometres. The maximum length of the entire race must not exceed 3,500 kilometres and there must be at least two rest days.

CONTINUED OVERLEAF ▶

Spain's Marino Lejarreta is the only rider to have completed all three Grand Tours in a season four times (in 1987, 1989, 1990 and 1991), but the rider who has completed the most consecutive Grand Tours is Australia's Adam Hansen (ten as of the Vuelta a España 2014). Only five riders have won all three Grand Tours – they are Eddy Merckx (of course), Bernard Hinault, Jacques Anquetil (who did it first), Felice Gimondi and Alberto Contador. No rider has ever won all three Grand Tours in a single year though Raphaël Géminiani (in 1955) and Gastone Nencini (in 1957) managed to finish in the top ten of all three races.

The Tour de France is the daddy of them all and continues to attract the world's best riders – it's the best-known cycle race and the biggest annual sporting event in the world and attracts a huge amount of international media attention. Though it sometimes seems to be the victim of its own success, it has a rich and lengthy history of myths and legends – a tapestry woven from courageous exploits and darker tales – but remains the race that all riders dream of winning. The Giro d'Italia is generally considered to be the tougher race, often ridden in terrible weather conditions ranging from burning sun to freezing snow, but has, until recently when rule changes led to international teams riding the race regularly, remained very much an Italian race. The Vuelta d'España, the new kid on the Grand Tour block, has always had something of an identity crisis, regularly changing its jerseys and its place in the calendar, where it's moved from being the first Grand Tour (in the spring, usually late April) to the last (now held in September) where it's often used as preparation for the world championships.

BLUFF FACT ► 'The Tour de France was first won by a Frenchman, Maurice Garin and the Giro d'Italia by an Italian, Luigi Ganna. But the first winner of the Vuelta a España was a Belgian, Gustaaf Deloor.'

BLUFF IT ► 'The Tour has the yellow jersey, the Giro has the pink jersey and the Vuelta has the orange ... no wait, white ... hang on, yellow ... er, gold ... no, definitely red jersey.' (The leader's jersey in the Vuelta has been all those colours over the years.)

GREGARIO

YOU SAY ► *GREE – GAR – EE – OH*
WHAT IT MEANS ► The *gregario* is the Italian equivalent of the *domestique* – those riders with no personal ambition who play 'follow the leader' in a bike race. From the Latin *grex* meaning a flock or herd, one of the greatest of the Italian *gregari* was Andrea Carrea who was Fausto Coppi's faithful lieutenant and the only rider ever to wish he had never worn the yellow jersey. In 1952, he got into a lucky break on stage 9 of the Tour de France and was informed at the finish line that he had taken the race lead. Utterly bewildered, Carrea burst into tears and had to be dragged to the podium for the jersey presentation, so unwilling was he to upstage his team leader. 'I heard I had inherited a jersey destined for champions. For me, it was a terrible situation,' he said later. Fortunately for the man who said 'we gave everything, even our souls, and it was still not enough', Coppi won the next day's stage, the first ever climb of the Alpe d'Huez, and wore the yellow jersey until the end of the race. Bartali's great *gregario* Giovannini Corrieri said it best: 'I have always been a *gregario*, a donkey, a horse with a cart to pull.' Without the sacrifice of his *gregari*, many a great champion might never have won a race.

H IS FOR ...

HINAULT Bernard

BORN ▸ 14 November, 1954, Yffiniac (Brittany), France

NATIONALITY ▸ French

ACTIVE ▸ 1975–1986

RIDER TYPE ▸ All-rounder, particularly strong in the time trials and aggressive in the mountains

NICKNAME ▸ The Badger

BIG WINS ▸ 5 × Tour de France (1978, 1979, 1981, 1982, 1985), 3 × Giro d'Italia (1980, 1982, 1985), 2 × Vuelta a España (1978, 1983), 2 × Liège–Bastogne–Liège (1977, 1980), 2 × Giro di Lombardia (1979, 1984), Paris –Roubaix (1981), world champion (1980)

MAJOR RIVALS ▸ Joop Zoetemelk, Laurent Fignon, Greg LeMond

Bernard Hinault is one of the great Breton riders – like first double Tour de France winner Lucien Petit-Breton and prolific Classics winner and first three-in-a-row Tour winner Louison Bobet – who came to dominate French cycling. As tough as the granite of the Breton coastline, as stubbornly independent as his fellow Celts, Hinault is second only to Eddy Merckx in terms of the breadth of his results and the single-minded determination to win every race he started, in emphatic style. Turning professional at 19, in 1974 – the last year of Merckx's dominance – Hinault won the Tour de France at his first attempt (in the French national champion's jersey and having already won the Vuelta), and then won it four more times in his relatively short career. The Frenchman rode the race eight times in total and never finished worse than second – the best record of any of the five-time winners' club. His *directeur sportif* Cyrille Guimard said he was the most talented rider he'd ever seen, including Merckx, and he might have achieved even greater feats than the Belgian had he

CONTINUED OVERLEAF ▸

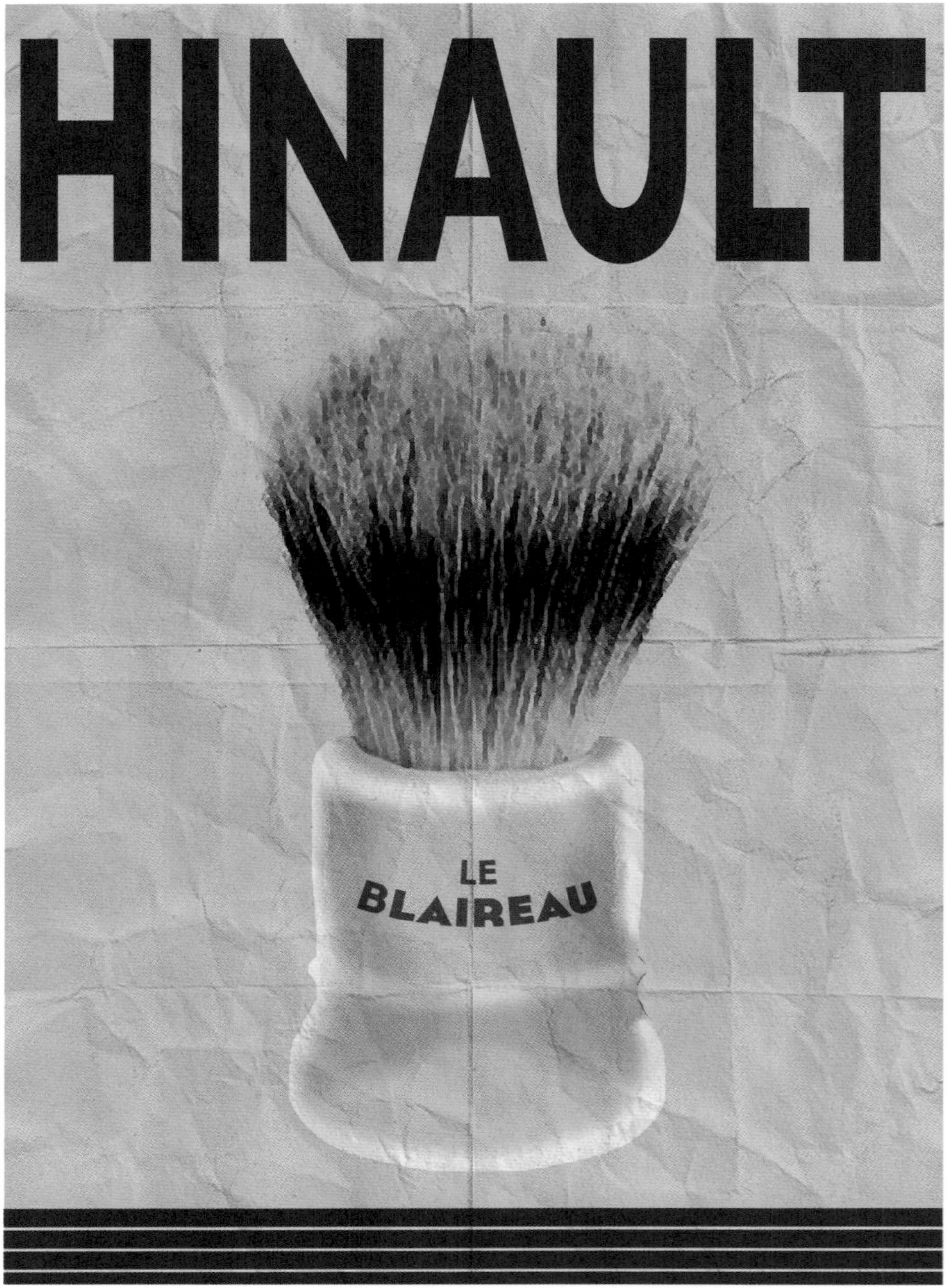
HINAULT
LE
BLAIREAU

not been plagued with knee trouble that caused him to withdraw from the 1980 Tour de France, when he was wearing the leader's yellow jersey.

Hinault's motto was 'as long as I breathe I attack' and his career was defined by four races – the 1980 Liège–Bastogne–Liège, ridden in a snowstorm, where Hinault attacked 80 kilometres from the finish and was ten minutes ahead of his nearest rival at the finish line; the 1981 Paris–Roubaix, a race that he famously called 'bullshit' but was determined to win anyway, and did, in the rainbow stripes of the world champion; the 1980 world championships where he simply devoured the opposition to win solo in a race that only 11 riders finished; and the 1986 Tour de France.

That latter race was promised to Greg LeMond, who had helped an injured Hinault to conquer his fifth win the year before. But instead of riding meekly in the peloton, the Breton attacked repeatedly – 'I race to win, not to please people' was another of his mantras – though he said he did so in order that his team-mate would have the satisfaction of having truly earned the victory. It was an enthralling race and Hinault cried when he gave up his last yellow jersey. The stage to Alpe d'Huez – when Hinault and LeMond ascended the twenty one hairpins side by side – is part of the legends of the Tour. The Frenchman would never ride the race again and retired later that year, aged 32. He remains the only rider to have won all three of the Grand Tours – the Tour, Giro and Vuelta – twice.

Today Hinault is part of the entourage of the Tour de France and can be seen on the podium after every stage congratulating the day's winner. Always a hugely combative rider the Frenchman was never averse to getting physical during the race, and there's a famous photo of him punching a protestor during the 1984 Paris–Nice. He has deployed the same skills several times in his post-race career, most famously in 2008 when he grappled a spectator off the winner's podium. Outside cycling, Hinault is a 'gentleman farmer' raising dairy cattle in his native Brittany.

> **BLUFF IT** ▸ *'Hinault suffered such severe frostbite in the 1980 Liège–Bastogne–Liège that two fingers on his right hand remain numb to this day.'*

HORS DÉLAI

YOU SAY ▸ *OR DAY – LAY*

WHAT IT MEANS ▸ As soon as the winner of a stage crosses the finish line, the clock is ticking. The *commissaires* will start to calculate *le délai* – in other words, the time limit inside which riders need to finish to stay in the race. If a rider or riders are *hors délai* they may be eliminated. The time delay is calculated as a percentage of the winner's time and the faster the winner is, the bigger the percentage. If more than 20 per cent of the peloton fall outside the time limit, then race organisers will review the situation, particularly if the delay has been caused by a crash. Particularly courageous individuals are often given a second chance. When Paul Sherwen (yes, the commentator) finished outside the time limit on stage 10 in the 1985 Tour de France, the *commissaires* allowed him to continue in the race. Why? Because, following a crash at the start of the stage, Sherwen rode 160 kilometres over six categorised climbs, alone, in his final Tour. Such guts and determination will soften even the hardest heart.

HORS CATÉGORIE

YOU SAY ► *OR CAT – EGG – OH – REE*

WHAT IT MEANS ► Have you ever heard a commentator talk about 'first cat climbs' as the riders hit the mountains? And wondered what cute furry domestic pets have to do with some of the toughest sporting challenges known to man? Climbs are categorised in cycling races as follows:

- Category 4: 100–300 metres
- Category 3: 300–600 metres
- Category 2: 600–1100 metres
- Category 1: 1100–1500 metres
- *Hors catégorie*: 1500 metres and above

But the categorisation of a climb can vary depending on where it comes in a stage (the later in the race, the higher the category) and how much race organisers want to incentivise riders to attack – categorisation of climbs is really about deciding how many points to award for the king of the mountains competition: the harder the climb, the bigger the number of points on offer. So why *hors catégorie* and not just Category 5? Think Spinal Tap, turning it up to 11 – the *hors catégorie* climbs are the toughest of the tough and saying they're 'beyond categorisation' just adds to their myth and mystique.

> **BLUFF IT** ► *'The story goes that climbs were originally categorised according to what gear a car needed to use to get up them – the* hors catégorie *climbs were the ones that a car couldn't get up at all.'*

RIDER

HOY Chris

BORN ► 23 March 1976, Edinburgh, Scotland
ACTIVE ► 1992–2013
BIG WINS ► 6 × Olympic gold (2004, 2008, 2012), 11 × world champion (variously team sprint, sprint, 1km time-trial and keirin: 2002, 2004, 2005, 2006, 2007, 2008, 2010, 2012), 2 × Commonwealth gold (2002, 2006)

Sir Christopher Andrew 'Chris' Hoy is the most successful Olympic cyclist of all time, Scotland's most successful Olympian and the British athlete with the most Olympic gold medals, all six of them, achieved in three successive Olympic Games. Hoy is a multi-talented athlete, having competed in rugby and rowing as well as cycling and holds a BSc in Applied Sports Science. Originally a pure power sprinter, specialising in the kilometre and team sprint events, Hoy developed the tactical ability to win in the individual sprint and keirin events, and he is a multiple gold medallist in these (the kilometre was discontinued as an Olympic event in 2008). Hoy is a multiple world champion and currently holds the world record for the flying 500-metre time trial (in a flying start event, cyclists are given a lap to build up momentum before being timed over the distance at maximum speed), set at altitude in La Paz, Bolivia in 2007. In 2008 he became the first British triple gold medallist in 100 years and was knighted for his achievement. His mother Carol, a nurse, received an MBE at the same ceremony. Retired from cycling since

2013, Sir Chris announced his intention to drive in the British GT championships with a view to driving in the Le Mans 24 Hours Race in 2016. Hugely competitive, the Scotsman says of himself 'Whether I'm racing bikes, racing cars, playing Monopoly, I'm always trying to win.'

BLUFF IT ► *'Chris Hoy was inspired to be a cyclist when he saw "E.T." at the age of six.'*

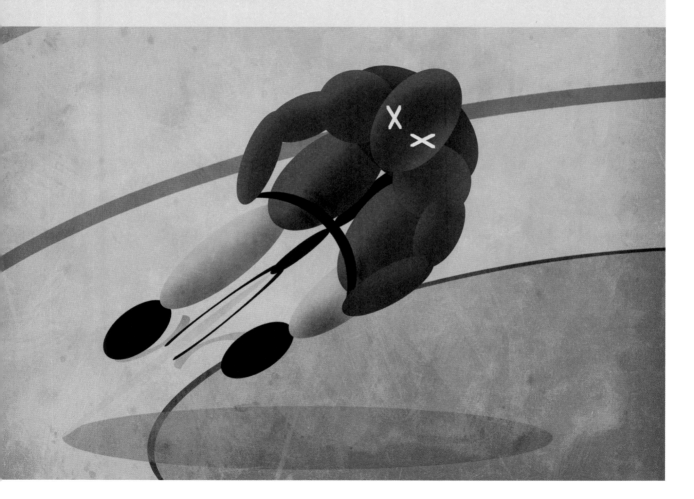

I IS FOR ...

INDURAIN Miguel

BORN ► 16 July 1964, Villava (Navarre), Spain
NATIONALITY ► Spanish
ACTIVE ► 1984–1996
RIDER TYPE ► All-rounder, completely dominant in the time trials and able to control the race in the mountains
NICKNAMES ► Big Mig, *le Roi Miguel*, *Miguelon*
BIG WINS ► 5 × Tour de France (1991–1995), 2 × Giro d'Italia (1992, 1993), Olympic time trial champion (1996), world time trial champion (1995), hour record (1994)
MAJOR RIVALS ► Tony Rominger, Alex Zulle

The gentle giant from Navarre was the fourth rider to win five Tours de France and the first to win them consecutively between 1991 and 1995. Indurain was widely believed to be something of a physiological freak of nature – with an at rest pulse rate of 28 beats per minute and a lung capacity of eight litres (the average person's is six) the big Spaniard (six foot two inches in cleats) was particularly well adapted to be a Grand Tour rider.

The humble champion with his crooked grin, luxuriant eyebrows and unflashy style would dictate the race by dominating the time trials, putting minutes into his rivals, and then controlling the race in the mountains – though he was quite capable of climbing with the best of them and won two stages in the Pyrenees before his reign at the Tour began. Often accused of lacking panache *(see P)* Indurain was ruthlessly efficient on the bike – winning back to back Giro/Tour doubles in 1992 and 1993 – yet the 'Sphinx of Pamplona' liked nothing better than to get back to the family farm and work on the land.

INNOVATION

From the earliest boneshakers to today's carbon-fibre superlight beauties, the design, components, materials and processes used to produce bicycles have been in a constant state of evolution. Though the essential components of a diamond-shaped frame and two equally sized wheels have remained constant since the creation of the Rover safety bicycle in Coventry in 1885, its inventor, John Kemp Starley, would be stunned by the innovations in the years since. Space-age materials like titanium and carbon fibre have made bikes stronger and lighter, while subtler upgrades like electronic gear shifting, asymmetric rings and disc brakes have improved operation and useability, and design specialisations have introduced bikes for specific types of riding like mountain biking. But the biggest innovations have come in the area of performance bikes and then trickled down to ordinary road-bike users: clipless pedals (Hinault used them on his way to 1985 Tour de France victory); quick-release mechanisms for changing wheels (Campagnolo introduced them in 1927); power meters (SRM developed the first commercial power meters in 1989, and they were quickly adopted by Greg LeMond) and triathlon bars (LeMond wasn't the first to use them but his winning time trial in the 1989 Tour de France bought them to popular attention). Modern developments like LED lights – more powerful, smaller and with a far superior battery life to conventional lights – and lycra – a lighter and more comfortable material for cycling gear, giving rise to the MAMIL (middle aged man in lycra) – have made cycling safer and more enjoyable for everyone.

BLUFF IT ▶ *'Do you know the innovative Lotus monocoque carbon fibre bike that Chris Boardman rode to a world record in the 1992 Barcelona Olympics was declared illegal because it didn't have a diamond shaped frame?*

When Indurain's Tour streak was broken by Bjarne Riis in 1996, he retired at the end of the season, though a scientific study published in 2012, after Indurain had undergone a battery of fitness tests, suggested that the Spaniard could still turn in a decent time trial if he wanted to. In 2003 Indurain said, 'If by magic I were going to ride the Tour, what would interest me most would be the prologue. It's the most emotive moment, where the tension accumulated during a year of work is released like a gunshot.'

BLUFF IT ▶ *'In the first time trial in the 1993 Tour de France there was an "Indurain Sandwich" – Miguel finished first and his brother Prudencio was dead last.'*

INTERMEDIATE SPRINT

A sprint during a stage that awards extra points for the points classification. There was a short-lived red jersey at the Tour (1971–1989) for the rider who accumulated the most points in the intermediate sprints. The Tour now has one 'supersprint' per stage with 20 bonus points on offer. The Giro d'Italia intermediate

CONTINUED OVERLEAF ▶

sprint competition was known as the Intergiro, but now all points count for the red jersey of the points classification. The intermediate sprints at the Giro also carry time bonuses, so it's not unusual to see general classification riders taking these on occasionally.

Time bonuses are also awarded for the intermediate sprints in the Vuelta a España and, because of the greater number of summit finishes, it's not unusual to see climbers taking the green jersey of the points classification.

IZOARD

ALTITUDE ▸ 2360 metres
HEIGHT GAIN ▸ 1438 metres
AVERAGE GRADIENT ▸ 4.5 per cent
MAXIMUM GRADIENT ▸ 8 per cent
LENGTH ▸ 31.7 kilometres
LOCATION ▸ French Alps

The Col d'Izoard is the true lunar landscape of the Tour. Where Alpe d'Huez twists its way through somewhat unattractive scrubland and Mont Ventoux blinds riders and spectators with its limestone whiteout, the *Casse Déserte* – the 'broken desert' – looks like the backdrop of a science-fiction movie – virtually nothing grows on its rubble strewn slopes, barren but for the strange free-standing stones, known as *cargneules* that rise up and reflect the changing of the light, casting their uncanny shadows come nightfall.

The list of winners on this fearsome climb – one of the highest passes in the Alps – reads like a who's who of the greats of the Tour de France and two of the greatest – Fausto Coppi and Lousin Bobet – are memorialised among the eerie standing stones of the *Casse Déserte*. It became synonymous with these two after their monopoly on the climb, either Coppi or Bobet winning the ascent of the Col d'Izoard between 1949 and 1954. It was Bobet – the

first man to win the Tour de France three times in a row, a feat he achieved between 1953 and 1955 – who said that reputations were made on the Izoard and that the mark of a true Tour de France champion was to lead the race from the front in the *maillot jaune* across that broiling rocky wilderness. Bobet did it himself three times, most notably on stage 18 in the 1953 Tour de France when he finished five minutes ahead of his rivals, watched by *il Campionissimo* himself, Fausto Coppi.

There is a small cycling museum at the summit and the pass is inaccessible in the winter. In 2011, Andy Schleck pulled off one of the great exploits of the modern sport when he rode for 60 kilometres alone – across the Izoard and then to the mighty heights of the Galibier, the highest ever finish in the Tour de France. Eddy Merckx was shouting encouragement from the team car and said afterwards, 'He rode with great courage, gave a cycling lesson to everybody.' High praise indeed from the greatest of them all.

BLUFF IT ▸ *'Coppi and Bobet may be the riders most associated with the Izoard, but it was a Belgian, Philippe Thys, who was first across the top when the Tour first used the climb in the 1922 race.'*

J IS FOR ...

JERSEY

A cycling jersey is a prize – the monobloc coloured jerseys that denote the leaders of the classifications in a stage race like the yellow and pink and amarillo jerseys of the three Grand Tours, the green or the white, red or blue or the iconic polka dots of the king of the mountains. But a cycling jersey is also a multicoloured billboard that bears every sponsor's name and creates the effect that the peloton is a gigantic living kaleidoscope of ever-shifting colour.

Some of the greatest of jerseys have been the simplest – the black and white chequerboard of Peugeot, the black banded ochre of Molteni, the blue of Alcyon and Bianchi or the plain, bold red of Saeco. Others have been inspired by modern art – the Mondrianesque La Vie Claire jersey – or pop art – the bold blue and red and white stripes of Brooklyn.

The first cycling jerseys were made of wool. Next came silk – lighter, cooler and far more stylish. The first silk jerseys were introduced in – where else – Italy in 1940. Then British chemists Dickson and Whinfield invented polyester in 1941 which was super absorbent, like wool, yet light and cool, like silk. Not to mention the fact that it could be printed with any colour combination you could dream of from the hyperkinetic multicoloured blocks of the iconic Mapei jersey to today's lime, pink and blue Lampre jersey, clearly designed by a 6-year-old girl.

The most famous cycling jerseys are the yellow jersey of the Tour de France, the pink jersey of the Giro d'Italia and the rainbow stripe jersey of the world champion.

BLUFF FACT ▸ Eddy Merckx is the only man to win all three jerseys – overall winner, points and mountains – in the Giro d'Italia in 1968 and the Tour de France in 1969. Two men have achieved the feat at the Vuelta – Tony Rominger in 1993 and Laurent Jalabert in 1995.

> **BLUFF IT** ▸ *'The Giro d'Italia used to award a* maglia nera *or black jersey for the last rider in the race between 1946 and 1951, a good 60 years before Rapha started the current trend for black jerseys.'*

LES MAILLOTS

K IS FOR ...

KING OF THE MOUNTAINS

You see that rider wearing the red and white polka dot jersey that looks like he has a case of the cartoon measles (particularly when accessorised with matching shorts, socks, shoes, sunglasses and even bike)? He is the king of the mountains – the rider who has accumulated the most points when crossing the great difficulties of a race. He wears red and white polka dots to take authority in the Alps, blue for dominating the Dolomites and blue and white polka dots for supremacy in the Sierras.

The king of the mountains – or *grand prix des montagnes* – is decided on points with the first rider over the summit of a climb taking the maximum points available. The bigger the mountain, the more points are available.

Spain's Federico Bahamontes is the outright king of the climbers with nine wins achieved in all three Grand Tours – six in the Tour de France, one in the Giro and two in the Vuelta. Belgium's Lucien Van Impe is one behind on eight wins, tied with Italy's Gino Bartoli. France's Richard Virenque *(see V)* holds the record for the Tour de France with seven wins achieved in the 1990s/2000s. Italy's Gino Bartali was seven times king of the mountains at the Giro and Spain's José Luis Laguía won the mountains prize at the Vuelta five times. Scotland's Robert Millar *(see M)* remains the only British winner of a king of the mountains jersey. Some of the greatest climbers came from the flatlands of Northern Europe – the 'Angel of the Mountains' Charly Gaul was from Luxembourg and Lucien Van Impe, renowned for his fluid style, was from Belgium.

But winning the king of the mountains jersey is not always the mark of the great climber. Italy's Marco Pantani only achieved the feat once, in 1998 at the Giro d'Italia when he won the race overall. Yet he is generally

CONTINUED OVERLEAF ▶

regarded as one of the greatest, if not *the* greatest, climbers of all time.

Obviously, women cyclists contest the 'queen of the mountains' and Britain's Dr Emma Pooley (she holds a doctorate in geotechnical engineering) is one of the greatest climbers in the women's peloton.

BLUFF FACT ▸ The first ever kings of the mountains were Spain's Vicente Trueba (Tour de France, 1933), Italy's Alfredo Binda (Giro d'Italia, 1933) and Italy's Edoardo Molinar (Vuelta a España, 1935)

BLUFF FACT ▸ Federico Bahamontes 'the Eagle of Toledo' flew up the Col de la Romeyere in the 1954 Tour de France then discovered he needed a wheel change when he got to the top. While he was waiting, he had time for an ice cream – that's how far ahead of the competition he was.

KEIRIN

Or 'the one with the moped' – the derny as it's known on the track. The keirin is a sprint event with up to nine riders in contention instead of two and with a furious no-holds-barred finish that often sees crashes as the race nears its thrilling conclusion – this is what happened to Sir Chris Hoy in the 2009 world championships.

It works like this: the black-clad derny (moped) rider paces the riders through the early laps of the race, gradually increasing the speed before he leaves the track with two laps to go. During this time riders jostle for position but they have to stay behind the derny's back wheel. But once the moped has left the track then it's every rider for themselves as they sprint for the win.

BLUFF FACT ▸ In Japan, where the keirin started, it's a hugely popular betting sport with millions of yen changing hands.

KELLY Sean

BORN ▸ 24 May, 1956, Carrick-on-Suir (Waterford), Ireland
NATIONALITY ▸ Irish
ACTIVE ▸ 1977–1994
RIDER TYPE ▸ Sprinter/all-rounder
NICKNAMES ▸ King Kelly, Sean (his real name is John James Kelly), Mr Paris–Nice, The New Cannibal (for his extraordinary 1984 season)
BIG WINS ▸ 4 × green jersey, Tour de France (1982, 1983, 1985, 1989); Vuelta a España (1988); 4 × points jersey, Vuelta a España (1980, 1985, 1986, 1988); 7 × Paris–Nice (1982, 1983, 1984, 1985, 1986, 1987, 1988); 2 × Milan–San Remo (1986, 1992); 2 × Paris–Roubaix (1984, 1986); 2 × Liège–Bastogne–Liège (1984, 1989); 3 × Giro di Lombardia (1983, 1985, 1991)
MAJOR RIVALS ▸ Eddy Merckx, Bernard Hinault, Greg LeMond, Laurent Fignon, Francesco Moser

John James 'Sean' Kelly is the greatest rider Ireland has produced. Although Stephen Roche *(see R)* pulled off the Triple Crown, Kelly's list of wins in shorter stage races like Paris–Nice and his Classics victories – winning all of the Monuments *(see M)* multiple times, except for the Tour of Flanders which evaded him (though he was second three times) – ranks him as one of the greatest riders of all time.

Kelly was the Irish farm boy whose sheer class and extraordinarily long career made him the match of the very greatest riders the sport has seen. With his 22 Classics wins he is statistically the fourth best of all time behind Merckx (50 wins), Hinault and Anquetil (29 wins apiece).

But greatness is about more than just the number of wins on a rider's *palmarès (see P)*. It's also about what you give back to the sport, and since his retirement, the Irishman has stayed actively involved establishing the Sean Kelly Racing Academy and the An Post professional cycling team. Kelly is also one of the voices of cycling, his droll and incisive commentary a great favourite of British fans.

Escaping a life of manual labour through his love of cycling, Kelly was a gifted amateur and turned pro at 18. But it was after he moved to France in 1977 that his career exploded. The young Irishman won a stage in his debut Tour de France that year and rapidly earned himself a reputation as a fearless sprinter, though not one capable of winning stage races. But his early team manager Jean de Gribaldy – who Kelly always said was ten years ahead of other *directeur sportifs (see D)* in his approach to diet and training, encouraging his riders to train smarter not harder – was a huge influence on the Irishman's career, employing him as a team leader who he believed could win stage races as well as sprints.

His faith was rewarded when Kelly triumphed in the 1982 Paris–Nice – the start of an unbroken, record run of seven wins in the event. This, coupled with his first green jersey at the Tour de France, rapidly changed minds and he finally nailed a Grand Tour win in 1988 taking the victory in a mountainous Vuelta a España thanks to his superior time-trialling skills and a little help from Scottish team-mate Robert Millar *(see M)*. Kelly's qualities as a rider, added to his abilities to excel in the worst conditions that nature could throw at him – made him a real contender for both the Classics and stage races.

His skills are best exemplified by his greatest exploits: the photo finish at the 1983 Giro di Lombardia, after Kelly had single-handedly closed down the gap to the front group then taken the tightest of sprints beating Greg LeMond and winning the first of his nine Monuments; his 1984 attack at Paris–Roubaix in foul weather conditions followed up by an equally aggressive ride at Liège–Bastogne–Liège to take his first wins in those races; his clever, tactical riding to take the yellow jersey for one day in 1983, taking the intermediate sprints and the final sprint finish to lead the race by one second; and of course his astonishing descent from the Poggio in the 1992 Milan–San Remo at the end of his illustrious career – flying down the hairpins like a madman he caught the race leader and then pummelled him in the sprint. Kelly once said, 'If you have a 100-metre lead at the top of the Poggio, you'll win.' That day he put the lie to his own words. It was the stuff of legend and a brilliant last hurrah to one of the most glittering careers in cycling.

BLUFF FACT ▶ At the end of the 1983 Tour de France, Kelly's car was broken into and the suitcase containing his yellow jersey was stolen. It was never returned. The framed jersey that now hangs alongside so many other mementoes of his career at his home in Ireland is a replica, provided by the Tour de France.

> **BLUFF IT** ▶ *'Of course Kelly is banned from the Olympics for life, after riding in South Africa in 1976 during the sport boycott. He was caught out when he was photographed with Richard Burton and Elizabeth Taylor and fans identified his photo in the Daily Mail.'*

L IS FOR ...

LANTERNE ROUGE

YOU SAY ▸ *LAN (rhymes with man) – TURN ROOZH (the final sound like the s in 'vision')*

The last rider to finish the Tour de France is called the *lanterne rouge*. Why the 'red lantern'? Guards on French trains used to hang a red lantern on the last carriage to signal that it was the end of the train. Between 1946 and 1951 the Giro gave the last rider in the race a black jersey, the *maglia nera*. You might not think that coming last was something to be proud of but some riders have taken it very seriously indeed – there are tales of riders jumping off and hiding until the peloton is minutes down the road before remounting in order to preserve their place at the bottom of the rankings. In the days before riders were paid decent salaries, being the *lanterne rouge* could guarantee good prize money on the lucrative post-Tour criterium circuit. So why do cycling fans love the *lanterne rouge*? Because he keeps riding to the *Champs-Élysées* even though he has no possible chance of winning. We admire his courage in just wanting to finish the greatest race in the world and for that he gets a *chapeau!*

BLUFF IT ▸ *'Edwig Van Hooydonck, lanterne rouge in 1993, won the Tour of Flanders twice – even great riders finish last.'*

LANTERNE ROUGE

LEAD OUT

When sprint speeds hit 60km/h plus, it's the lead-out man who's at the head of the race, driving the sprint train and hoping to launch his sprinter to the finish line to raise his arms in the V of victory. Easily capable of winning races in his own right, his job is to steer his designated sprinter through the minutest of gaps into pole position as the race hurtles over the final kilometres towards the finish line. A well-drilled lead-out train will keep the pace high, discourage late attacks and allow their sprinter to dive off the wheel at the last possible moment to deliver win after win. But one false move can spell disaster, leaving you at the bottom of a heap of riders after a spectacular crash. The great Italian sprinter Mario Cipollini was the first rider to use a sprint train in the late 1980s and early 1990s when the red jerseys of his Saeco team helped him to dominate sprinting with his famous 'Red Train'. Britain's Mark Cavendish – the Manx Missile – has elevated the sprint train to a fine art, helping him to dominate sprinting in recent years.

> **BLUFF IT** ▶ *'Of course Mark Renshaw is the best lead-out man in the business.' (Australian rider Renshaw is Mark Cavendish's lead-out man.)*

RIDER

LEMOND Greg

BORN ▸ 26 June, 1961, Lakewood (California), United States

NATIONALITY ▸ American

ACTIVE ▸ 1981–1994

RIDER TYPE ▸ All-rounder with strong climbing and time-trialling ability

NICKNAMES ▸ The American, the Monster, the Cowboy

BIG WINS ▸ 3 × Tour de France (1986, 1989, 1990), 2 × world champion road race (1983, 1989)

MAJOR RIVALS ▸ Bernard Hinault, Laurent Fignon

Gregory James LeMond was the first – and now the only – American to win the Tour de France. But he will always be best remembered for beating Frenchman Laurent Fignon in the 1989 Tour de France by eight seconds or 82 metres after a 3285 km race. He was the complete rider with the total skill set for Grand Tour success demonstrating both climbing and time-trialling ability from an early age. He was third in his first Tour de France in 1984, riding, ironically, in support of Fignon,

then switched to riding for Bernard Hinault in 1985. If 1989 is widely acknowledged to be the greatest Tour ever, 1986 can lay good claim to the title too, showcasing as it did the rivalry between the two team-mates – the older Frenchman going for a record sixth Tour de France and the young American aiming to win his first – culminating in their epic side-by-side ride up Alpe d'Huez. LeMond was at the height of his career when, in 1987, he was accidentally shot in a hunting accident. Minutes from death, he only returned to racing at the highest level in 1989 and the rest is history – his eight-second triumph on the *Champs-Élysées* capped one of the greatest sporting comebacks of all time.

BLUFF IT ▸ *'Of course LeMond was one of the great innovators – the first million-dollar rider and the man who introduced tribars to the sport.' (In case you're wondering, tribars are the additional handlebars now widely used in time trialling to give a more aerodynamic position – he used them in 1989 and Fignon didn't, which made all the difference.)*

LIÈGE–BASTOGNE –LIÈGE

WHERE ▶ Belgium (Ardennes)

TYPE OF RACE ▶ One-day Classic

NICKNAME ▶ *La Doyenne* (the Old Lady – Liège–Bastogne–Liège is the oldest of the Monuments)

TERRAIN ▶ Rolling countryside with short, sharp climbs including La Redoute, Côte de Saint Nicolas and the Stockeu

TIME OF YEAR ▶ Spring

MULTIPLE WINS ▶ Eddy Merckx (again!) won the race five times

MOST WINS BY COUNTRY ▶ Perhaps not surprisingly, Belgium

GREAT MOMENTS ▶ The 1980 race took place in a snowstorm – after an hour, half of the 174 riders who had started the race had abandoned. Bernard Hinault won after riding 80 kilometres alone through arctic conditions that left him with loss of feeling in his hands but his victory is widely acknowledged to be one of the greatest Classics exploits of all time.

Liège–Bastogne–Liège is the Walloon equivalent of the Tour of Flanders – its route sticks to the French-speaking areas of Southern Belgium and in particular the Ardennes. *La Doyenne* is the jewel in the crown of the Ardennes Classics week that starts with the Amstel Gold and moves on to Flèche-Wallonne with its ascent of the Mur de Huy, that reaches an astonishing 26 per cent gradient over 1km.

La Doyenne offers nothing quite as steep but its climbs, like La Redoute with steep sections of 15 per cent, recur with almost metronomic

frequency – this is a race of elimination, with only the very strongest in contention by the time the race finishes in the suburbs of Ans.

The race winds through the dense woods and ancient hills of the Ardennes, through an area that was once one of the industrial powerhouses of Europe. A huge Italian ex-pat population, whose grandfathers emigrated to work in the mining industry, turns out every year, and they've had plenty to cheer about with Moreno Argentin's three back-to-back wins in the 1980s and Michele Bartoli's pair of wins in the 1990s. But it is Merckx who is the undisputed king of *La Doyenne*, with his five wins. In recent years the race has become a truly international affair with winners from the USA, Spain, Luxembourg, Kazakhstan, Ireland and Australia.

BLUFF IT ▶ *'The Stockeu climb has a statue of Eddy Merckx at the top – he always launched his race winning attacks at that point.'*

M IS FOR ...

MERCKX Eddy

BORN ▸ 17 June, 1945, Tielt-Winge (Flemish Brabant), Belgium

NATIONALITY ▸ Belgian

ACTIVE ▸ 1965–1978

RIDER TYPE ▸ Capable of anything on the road and the track

NICKNAME ▸ The Cannibal

BIG WINS ▸ Too many to list – Merckx won every major race in the sport, at least once, and holds the outright record for number of Grand Tour (11) and Classics (19) wins

MAJOR RIVALS ▸ None, he was quite simply the greatest rider of all time

What is there to say about Edouard Louis Joseph, Baron Merckx? In his pomp (1965–1975) he won 35 per cent of all the races he entered including 11 Grand Tour victories and he is the only rider ever to win all the jersey classifications – overall, points and mountains – at the Giro (1968) and the Tour de France (1969), the latter at his first attempt.

Merckx's ride in the 1969 Tour is the most dominant ever. He pulled off one of the greatest exploits the race has ever seen as well, when he attacked in the Pyrenees and rode alone over the great climbs of the Tourmalet and the Aubisque for 105 kilometres, finally finishing eight minutes ahead of his closest rival. What was most astonishing was that Merckx didn't need to do it – he was already comfortably ahead in the race by that point and could simply have kept an eye on his closest rivals. But that wasn't Merckx's way – they didn't call him the Cannibal for nothing. His record of 525 victories will never be bettered.

Merckx decided to become a professional cyclist aged eight, though nothing in his bourgeois

CONTINUED OVERLEAF ▸

background suggested that the young Belgian would earn a living riding a bike, let alone become the greatest cyclist of them all. He called it 'a vocation', saying, 'I got enormous pleasure simply from riding a bike. So I guess racing was a reason for riding it more. Later I raced a lot because it was my métier. It was where I felt confident, where I was Eddy Merckx. I loved to race. In races it was just me, the bike and the race. It was a joy.' But the Belgian maintains he never raced to be the best, simply for the enjoyment of cycling – and to win. He still rides around 60 kilometres a week, but with friends and a glass of wine afterwards.

Merckx was an occasional smoker – he said it relaxed his lungs – and often needed a chair in the shower after races, such was his fatigue and the level of effort he would put in. For Merckx, winning was everything and such was his appetite for success that he would drive himself to exhaustion and sometimes use threats and intimidation to get what he wanted. The ultimate *patron (see P)*, in the 1974 Tour he refused to allow one of the sprinters to take the *maillot jaune* early in the race, stating baldly, 'it's my yellow jersey'. Psychologically impenetrable, mentally as hard as iron and with the physiological ability to accomplish anything on a bike that he set his mind to, Merckx was,

quite simply, the most accomplished rider ever to turn a pedal – as capable of winging through the mountains as Fausto Coppi and of dominating the time trials as Jacques Anquetil.

The truly astonishing thing about the Belgian's subsequent career is that he rode for the rest of his life in enormous pain – a crash in a track race in France left him with head, spinal and pelvic injuries (it was a race paced by a derny or small motorbike – the driver was killed). He claimed he was never as strong again in the mountains and that, had he not crashed, he would have won more races including more Tours de France. Even so, he still holds the record for most stage wins and most yellow jerseys.

BLUFF FACT ▶ Britain's Barry Hoban liked to tell the following story: 'Did you know that Poulidor and Gimondi each copped a 50-franc fine for taking a tow from a truck? And what was Merckx doing? He was towing the truck.' Similar tales have been told down the years about all cycling's hard men – there's a whole website devoted to similar tales about Germany's Jens Voight.

BLUFF IT ▶ *'When Merckx dominated the 1969 Tour they coined a word for it* – Merckxissimo.*'*

MARMOLADA/PASSO FEDAIA

YOU SAY ▸ *MAR – MO – LAH – DAH*
ALTITUDE ▸ 2057 metres
HEIGHT GAIN ▸ 1059 metres
AVERAGE GRADIENT ▸ 7.5 per cent
MAXIMUM GRADIENT ▸ 9 per cent
LENGTH ▸ 14 kilometres
LOCATION ▸ Dolomites, Italy

Though the Marmolada is the highest peak in the *Dolomiti,* the *Passo Fedaia* that crosses it is not the longest or the hardest of climbs, though its long uphill straights can seem endless.

It was here in 1998 that Marco Pantani attacked Swiss rider Alex Zulle and finished over four minutes ahead of him by the end of that day in the high Dolomites, the Swiss cracking under the pressure. Pantani went on to win the Giro/Tour double that year. Here that Spain's Miguel Indurain secured his second Giro d'Italia win in 1993, when Italian climber Bugno blew up, going too hard on its interminable slopes, and the big Spaniard set a relentless pace to reel him back in.

And it was here, in 1987, that one of the most dramatic days in modern bike racing was played out in a stage that has become known as the 'Marmolada massacre'. It started the day before, on the 225-kilometre stage from Lido di Jesolo to Sappada. Stephen Roche *(see R)* attacked the pink jersey – a legitimate tactic, except the race leader was his team-mate Roberto Visentini, the 1986 champion. There was a vicious rivalry and dislike between the two men, and Roche felt he deserved to be the team leader at the Giro. Visentini, the defending champion, disagreed – he felt he had the right to defend his title. The enmity was allowed to develop unchecked – Visentini declared he would help Roche to win the Tour de France in return for the Irishman's loyalty at the Giro d'Italia, even though Visentini hated the Tour. This kind of arrangement is not unusual between two strong teammates – think Hinault and LeMond in the 1986 Tour de France or Wiggins and Froome riding for Sky in 2012.

It went like this: The Italian had already declared he would attack Roche if necessary to win the race, so Roche attacked first, on stage 15, and refused to ease back even when his *directeur sportif (see D)* sent the rest of his team to pull him back. Visentini limped over the line some six minutes behind the insubordinate Irishman. Roche was in the lead and the whole of Italy hated him. He set out on stage 16, which ended with the climb of the Marmolada, flanked by his faithful *gregario (see G)* Belgian Eddy Schepers, Scotland's Robert Millar *(see M)* and Australia's Phil Andersen. He endured the entire 214-kilometre stage being spat at, jostled, jeered and punched by the enraged *tifosi (see T)*. Visentini boasted about his attempts to cause Schepers to crash and launched attack after attack, with Roche marking his every move. Having weathered the barrage of abuse, Roche crossed the finish line in the same time as Visentini. The stage – and the battle for team leadership and the pink jersey – were over.

> **BLUFF IT** ▸ *'Lago Fedaia, the lake at the foot of the Marmolada, was used as a location in the remake of the Italian Job.'*

MADISON

The Madison – named after Madison Square Gardens in New York City where the race was invented in the 1890s (the French call it *l'Americaine* or the American) – is basically a points race *(see O for Omnium)* with two important differences:

- The race is contested by two-person teams.
- Any team that laps the field is automatically in the winning position, regardless of how many points they have.

The Madison started life as an event in the popular and highly lucrative six-day events where riders would compete day and night and often suffer the effects of extreme exhaustion. When a law was passed in 1897 limiting the number of hours that a rider could be on the track, the idea of a team event where one rider could take a breather quickly gained traction.

The real highlight of the Madison is the changeover between riders – while the racing is in full swing at the bottom of the velodrome, the riders taking a breather circle high on the banking until their team-mate grabs their hand and catapults them into the thick of the action. The handsling is one of the trickiest manoeuvres in track racing and is utterly spectacular when done well. Confusing, chaotic and dramatic, the Madison is definitely not a race for the faint-hearted.

MAGIC SPANNER

Just like the sticky bottle *(See S)*, the magic spanner appears from the team car to tinker with a rider's bike and seems to take forever to make a repair while, in the meantime, the rider holds onto the car roof and takes a welcome breather.

MAILLOT

YOU SAY ► *MY – OH*

WHAT IT MEANS ► The French word for jersey *(see J)*

> **BLUFF IT** ► *'Lance Armstrong used to be known as Mellow Johnny, because that's how the Americans pronounce* maillot jaune *(the French for yellow jersey)'.*

MARVINGT Marie

In 1908, 110 men stood on the start line of the Tour de France in Paris. Twenty-seven days later, only 36 men finished the race ... and one woman – Marie Marvingt, danger's sweetheart: aviatrix, fencer, runner, swimmer, boxer, skier, martial artist, one of the best Alpine climbers in the world (inventing and wearing culottes because she was forbidden to climb in trousers), record holder in multiple sports who, aged 86, rode the 280 kilometres from her home in Nancy to Paris to gain her helicopter pilot's licence. In the course of her long and extraordinary life she also fought in the trenches in the First World War, became the world's first female fighter pilot and invented the air ambulance service, becoming France's most decorated woman with the *Croix de Guerre* and the *Legion d'Honneur*.

Of course she was refused official entry to the race – she was told in no uncertain terms that the Tour de France was an event for men only. But, undeterred, she set off shortly after the men and rode the same 14-stage 4488 km route including the climbs of the Ballon d'Alsace, the Col de Porte and the Côte de Laffrey. In 1909 a letter to *l'Auto* asked when there would be a women's Tour de France? The response: when the mountains of France have been flattened. But mountains didn't stop Marie Marvingt from becoming the first woman to ride the Tour de France.

MECHANIC

AKA 'tech' and 'wrench'. Keeps riders bikes tweaked to perfection, making repairs and adjustments as necessary and wielding the magic spanner *(see M)* mid-race when necessary. Ernesto Colnago *(see Q for Quick Release)* was Merckx's mechanic at his all-conquering Molteni team and continues to innovate bicycle mechanics in his 80s.

> **BLUFF IT** ▶ *'Bicycle mechanics have had a huge impact on modern technology – Henry Ford was a bike mechanic and so were the Wright Brothers who built their first plane out of lightweight bicycle components.'*

MECHANICAL

When a rider 'has a mechanical' it means something has gone wrong with his bike – most usually a problem with the chain or the gears. Not to be confused with having a puncture. Nowadays when a rider has a mechanical he will usually grab a replacement bike or spend some time having adjustments made with the 'magic spanner' *(see M)*.

BLUFF FACT ▶ In the 1963 Tour de France, before bike changes were permitted, Jacques Anquetil wanted to use a different bike on the descent of the Col de la Forclaz. Anquetil's *directeur sportif (see D)* Raphaël Géminiani arranged for him to have a 'mechanical' by getting a mechanic to cut Anquetil's derailleur cable. The Frenchman was able to make a legitimate bike change and by the time the *commissaires* got round to inspecting his original bike, the repair had been made. Anquetil went on to win his fourth Tour in a row.

MILLAR Robert

BORN ▶ 13 September, 1958, Glasgow, Scotland
NATIONALITY ▶ Scottish
ACTIVE ▶ 1980–1995
RIDER TYPE ▶ Specialist climber
NICKNAME ▶ Diffi (according to Millar, this is the nickname he would have given himself)
BIG WINS ▶ Tour de France king of the mountains (1984), Giro d'Italia king of the mountains (1987), Tour of Catalonia (1985), Dauphiné Libéré (1990), national road race champion (1995)
MAJOR RIVALS ▶ Pedro Delgado

Scotland's Robert Millar was the first British rider ever to win the king of the mountains at the Tour and the Giro and so very nearly becoming the first Briton to win a Grand Tour finishing second in the 1985 and 1986 Vuelta a España and the 1987 Giro d'Italia. Coupled with his fourth place at the 1984 Tour de France, he is the only British rider to have finished in the top five in all three Grand Tours. His second place at the Giro is the closest a Briton has come to winning the illustrious Italian race.

A gifted climber, Millar won a huge stage in the Pyrenees in his debut Tour de France in 1983. The Scotsman had moved to Paris in 1979 and promptly won the *Merlin Plage*, the trophy for the best amateur of the season, earning him a professional contract with the Peugeot team. Millar was only 23 when he raised his arms aloft on that stage to Pau in 1983, beating future Tour winner Pedro Delgado in the process. And he kept getting better. The next year, he shone again in the Tour, taking another monster stage in the Pyrenees finishing at the climb to the ski station in Guzet-Neige and winning the polka dot jersey of the king of the mountains, still the only Briton to do so. His fourth place finish was only surpassed by Bradley Wiggins (third in 2009 when Lance Armstrong was disqualified and winner in 2012) and Chris Froome (winner 2013).

Now Millar was talked of as a prospective Grand Tour champion and the following year, at the 1985 Vuelta a España, he seemed set to become the first Briton to win one of the biggest prizes in the sport. Wearing the leader's jersey, he started the penultimate stage with a 10-second cushion over Francisco Rodríguez, the Colombian riding for the Spanish Zor team. Knowing he only had to mark his rival over the three major climbs of the day to mark the biggest win of his life, he stuck to the South American like glue until a puncture on the second ascent of the day left Millar chasing back to the leaders. When the catch was made, on the final climb of the day, Rodríguez congratulated the young Scot on his great success ...

What Millar didn't know, and what Rodríguez was careful not to tell him, was that the Spaniard Pedro Delgado – who had started the stage in sixth place some six minutes behind the Scot but who was riding on roads he knew like the back of his hand in his home region of Castile y Leon – had attacked and was currently the leader on the road. Millar – without a team-mate owing to the fact that they had been held up at a level crossing for a train that never arrived – lost the race by 36 seconds. It was forever after known as the 'stolen Vuelta' for the outright collusion between the Spanish teams,

though Millar also blamed his own *directeur sportif (see D)* for not organising enough support from the non-Spanish teams.

Although Millar allegedly said he would never return to Spain, he was back at the race again the next year and, despite taking the leader's jersey again after a fine stage win, finished second again, this time behind Spain's Álvaro Pino. In 1987, he debuted at the Giro, taking the mountain jersey on stage 1B and never relinquishing it for the rest of the race. He also aligned himself with Stephen Roche *(see R)*, who had earned the enmity of the Italian fans – and lost the support of his own team – when he attacked his team leader to take the race lead. Perhaps the Scot was remembering his own experiences at the hands of the Spanish riders in the 1985 Vuelta.

Always shy and reclusive, the taciturn Scot was an introvert and loner who eventually retired from the sport in 1995 after his French *Le Groupement* team went bust. He has coached national teams and continues to work as a cycling journalist, his incisive and pithy columns gracing websites like cyclingnews.com. But his huge climbing talent and his achievements in the high mountains have ensured him a place in the pantheon of the all-time great climbers.

BLUFF FACT ▸ When Millar married Frenchwoman Sylvie Transler in 1985, his teammate Australian Phil Anderson said, 'he didn't seem to have the skills for getting on with men, let alone women'.

MILAN–SAN REMO

TYPE OF RACE ▶ One-day Classic

WHERE ▶ Italy

NICKNAME ▶ *La Primavera*

TERRAIN ▶ Flat with a series of rolling climbs towards the finish

TIME OF YEAR ▶ Early spring (though between 1937–1981 it was held on 19 March, St Joseph's Day, an important national holiday in Italy)

MULTIPLE WINS ▶ Eddy Merckx won seven times

MOST WINS BY COUNTRY ▶ Not surprisingly, Italy

GREAT MOMENTS ▶ Sean Kelly's extraordinary attack on the descent from the Poggio to reel in Moreno Argentin and win the 1992 race; Oscar Freire snatching victory by three centimetres from Erik Zabel as the latter started to celebrate the victory in 2004; the heavy snow and arctic conditions that saw the 2013 race shortened by the organisers and the riders taken over the most difficult part of the route by bus; Mark Cavendish rocketing out of the pack to win in 2009 when it seemed that Heinrich Haussler had the victory sewn up.

Milan–San Remo may not be the hardest of the Classics, but at close to 300 kilometres, it is the longest. From its first edition in 1907 up until 1960 it was a sprinter's Classic. The now iconic climbs of the Poggio and the Cipressa were added in 1960 and 1982 to try and break the fast men's supremacy, especially the foreign sprinters like Rik Van Steenbergen who dominated the race in the 1950s. His victory in 1954 over Fausto Coppi, Gino Bartali and Louison Bobet is considered to be the finest sprint finish ever at the race. Instead the addition of those rolling climbs so close to the finish line gave rise to a different type of winner as the Classics specialists began to dominate with Eddy Merckx winning the race a record seven times between 1966 and 1976.

La Primavera is the also the first and earliest of the Classics and the weather has often been dreadful. In 1910 only four riders finished the race, and the winner, France's Eugene Christophe, was hospitalised for a month until he regained the full use of his arms and legs. And, being an Italian race, it also saw one of Fausto Coppi's legendary exploits. In 1946 he attacked at the top of the Turchino climb and rode 145 kilometres to the finish on the Via Roma alone, over 14 minutes ahead of his rivals. What made it all the more extraordinary was that Coppi had been in a British prisoner of war camp until 1945.

But despite the tinkering with the route, the Milan–San Remo remains defiantly a race for the sprinters and has featured on the *palmarès* of all the boy racers who have graced the sport over the years.

BLUFF FACT ▶ Milan–San Remo was modelled on a car race and set out to prove that it was physically possible to ride a bicycle over the same distance.

BLUFF IT ▶ *'No rider has ever won three times in a row – German sprinter Erik Zabel came closest when he came first-first-second in 1997–1999.'*

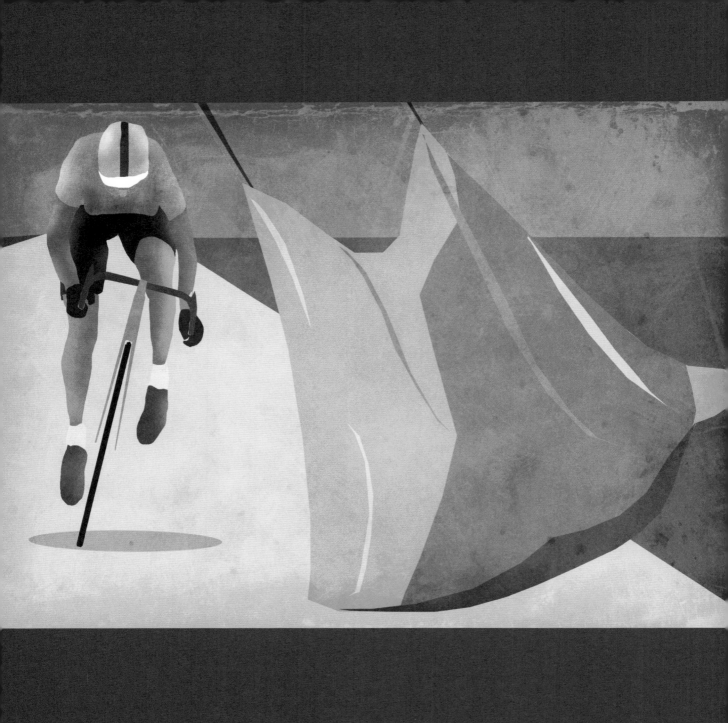

MORTIROLO

YOU SAY ► *MORE – TEA – ROLO*
ALTITUDE ► 1852 metres
HEIGHT GAIN ► 1300 metres
AVERAGE GRADIENT ► 10.5 per cent
MAXIMUM GRADIENT ► 18 per cent
LENGTH ► 12.4 kilometres
LOCATION ► Dolomites, Italy

Along with the equally fearsome Stelvio, the Mortirolo is one of the giants of Italian climbing. A regular feature of the Giro d'Italia since 1990, there is a monument to Italy's greatest climber Marco Pantani eight kilometres from the finish. Since 2004 there has been a special *Cima Pantani* (Pantani summit prize) awarded to the first rider over the top in memory of the Italian who made his name there when he launched a spectacular attack at the foot of the climb in the 1994 Giro.

> **BLUFF IT** ► *'With an average gradient of 10.5 per cent, riding the Mortirolo is like riding up the side of the Pyramids.'*

MONUMENT

The nickname given to one of the 'big five' Classics races, the oldest and most celebrated one-day races in the sport (for a list of the Monuments *see C for Classics*). Outside the Grand Tours *(see G)*, these are the races all cyclists want on their *palmarès (see P)*.

MOTO

The motorcycle riders who risk life and limb to bring TV coverage from the peloton and provide riders with time checks on a blackboard. Not to be confused with 'Motoman' who ferried EPO and other performance-enhancing drugs to Lance Armstrong.

MUSETTE

YOU SAY ► *MEW – SET*
WHAT IS IT? ► You know that moment in a race when the riders slow down and grab a small bag from someone standing in the middle of the road risking life and limb to hand them out? Those bags are *musettes*, small, light cloth bags packed with a rider's lunch. So what's in a typical musette? The baguettes and *patisseries* of old have been replaced by energy bars and gels, fresh-made rice cakes, dried fruit, bananas, water and energy drinks – but the odd can of Coke and fruit cake still sneak in. Like *bidons*, discarded *musettes* make great race souvenirs.

N IS FOR ...

NATURAL BREAK

Let's face it, we've all wondered how cyclists can ride for hundreds of kilometres, for hours at a time, without needing a pee. The fact is they can't and don't. They take a 'natural break'. This often happens by arrangement in which case most of the peloton stops and lines up by the side of the road wherever there's a convenient hedge. Occasionally you'll see riders performing the 'in flight' manoeuvre – sliding out through the short's leg with a pelvic thrust and a knee flick to avoid splashback assisted by a team-mate's steadying hand. Cameramen are generally polite or prudish enough to avert the camera's gaze and there's an unwritten rule that you don't attack a rider when's he off the bike for a 'natural break'. But like all the best unwritten rules it's regularly broken. Louison Bobet attacked Charly Gaul when he was having a pee during the 1951 Giro and pinched the stage from him. Gaul earned the nickname 'Cheri Pipi' for that one. And in 2000, Laurent Jalabert was left floundering when a breakaway took advantage of his taking a natural break. The French press quickly dubbed it 'the affair of the piss pot', but Jalabert lost the yellow jersey as a result. As a last resort you can always do it in your shorts. Aim to be going downhill and not into a headwind so you don't get blowback. And never do it when you're wearing legwarmers.

BLUFF FACT ▶ For number twos a cycling cap down the back of the shorts is the preferred option.

BLUFF FACT ▶ Top women's cyclist Marijn de Vries has a technique she calls the 'quick pee' – a way of gaining maximum relief for minimum exposure.

BLUFF FACT ▶ Eighteen riders were banned from riding a race in the New Forest because they peed by the side of the road and not in the toilets provided.

NEFFATI Ali

In 1913, an 18-year-old Tunisian rode the Tour de France – in a fez. Like Tommy Cooper. And Neffati had a sense of humour to match: he told Henri Desgrange, who thought he might be suffering on a particularly hot and humid day, 'Oh, Monsieur Desgrange, I'm freezing!' Not surprisingly, the young Tunisian became the darling of the peloton. He wouldn't have been at the race at all were it not for the great and the good of Tunisian sport. Boxers, fencers and track cyclists organised a gala for his benefit on 7 June, 1913, and 16 days later he was on the start line in Paris, ready to ride into Tour history. He never finished the Tour – he abandoned on stage 4, rode again a year later and was hit by a race organiser's car, abandoning on stage 8 – but he went on to carve out a lucrative career on the tracks of France, Italy and the USA. So, for Ali Neffati *chapeau* – a red, tasselled one if you like.

NICKNAMES

Every rider worth his salt has a nickname. They range from the straightforward – Wiggo (Bradley Wiggins) – to the downright bizarre. French rider Jean Robic was known variously as the 'Yellow Dwarf', 'Biquet' (the goat), 'Tête de Cuir' (leatherhead, from the old fashioned padded leather helmet he wore as a result of breaking his skull in Paris–Roubaix) and 'the Hobgoblin of the Brittany Moor'. Nicknames come from a rider's physical appearance – Octave Lapize was known as 'Frisé' (Curly, for his mop of ringlets) – their achievements – Roger de Vlaeminck was known as 'Mr Paris Roubaix' after his success in that race – or in-jokes – Cadel Evans is 'Cuddles' in contrast to his notoriously prickly racing temperament. Eddy Merckx was, not surprisingly, 'the Cannibal' for his appetite for winning races, though it was his team-mate's young daughter who came up with the name.

Climbers' nicknames often reflect their ability to soar at altitude – 'the Eagle of Toledo' (Frederico Bahamontes), the 'Angel of the Mountains' (Charly Gaul), 'the Eagle of Vizille' (Thierry Claveyrolat), 'the Heron' (Fausto Coppi). Sprinters, not surprisingly, have boy-racer nicknames like 'AleJet' (Alessandro Petacchi), 'The Tashkent TGV' (Djamolidine Abdoujaparov), 'Tornado Tom' (Tom Boonen) and the 'Manx Missile' (Mark Cavendish). The heavyweight *rouleurs* have nicknames that reflect their ability to roll over any obstacle – Tony Martin is 'der Panzerwagon', Fabian Cancellara is 'Spartacus', Bram Tankink is simply 'the Tank'.

Then there are the animals – Bernard Hinault was 'the Badger' supposedly for his ferocity as a competitor, Paolo Bettini was 'the Cricket' for his small stature and explosive power when he attacked, Mario Cipollini was 'the Lion King' for the way he roared to the finish in a sprint and there are plenty of tiny Spanish riders who've been nicknamed 'Flea'. And not forgetting the professions – Luis Herrera was 'the Little Gardener', Maurice Garin 'the Little Sweep', Ottavio Bottecchia 'the bricklayer from Friuli' based on the jobs they did before becoming professional cyclists.

BLUFF FACT ▶ Not only did Colombian climber Roberto Buitrago have the nickname 'Little Bird' but his team truck had a nickname too – 'the Birdcage'.

O IS FOR ...

OMNIUM

This is a multi-discipline track-cycling event, a bit like the decathlon in athletics. It's a great test of a rider's all-round abilities as the winner needs speed, strength and endurance and to be able to sprint, time trial and ride tactically in a bunch. The men's and women's omnium replaced the individual pursuit, the points race and the Madison at the 2012 Olympics. The six events are:

■ **Flying time trial:** as the name suggests, riders build up speed by riding on the top of the banking of the velodrome, then fly down to the bottom of the track and go hell for leather over 250 metres. Best time wins.

■ **Points race:** a long-distance race, where a sprint is held every 10 laps. Points are awarded to the top four finishers (5, 3, 2 and 1) and the rider with the most points at the finish wins. If you're strong enough, or canny enough, you can lap the field and grab yourself 20 points.

■ **Elimination race:** devil take the hindmost – at the end of every lap or every set number of laps, the last rider to cross the line is eliminated. Bye.

■ **Individual pursuit** *(see P)*.

■ **Scratch race:** all riders start together and the winner is the first one across the line at the end of the race. There are no points or intermediate sprints – it's the track equivalent of a road race. One for the endurance riders.

■ **Time trial** *(see T)*.

For each event one point is awarded for the winner, two for second place, three for third and so on. The overall winner of the omnium is the rider with the lowest number of points at the end of all six events.

OFF THE FRONT/BACK

This one is self-explanatory – if you're off the front you're on the attack, if you're off the back, you're in trouble.

ON THE RIVET

Or working flat out during a race – old-fashioned leather saddles had a rivet at the front and when you were working as hard as you could you were actually sitting 'on the rivet'.

OPPERMAN
Sir Hubert

'Oppy' Opperman wasn't the first Australian to ride the Tour de France – that honour goes to Donald Kirkham and Ivor 'Snowy' Munro who chanced their arm at the 1914 race – or the first to wear the yellow jersey or win that illustrious race – those honours fell to Phil Anderson 'the Kangaroo' in 1981 and Cadel Evans in 2011 – or even the first to win one of the Monuments of cycling – that was Stuart O'Grady when he crossed the finish line of the 2007 Paris–Roubaix – but without Oppy, Australian wouldn't be the cycling nation it is today with its own powerhouse 'superteam' Orica-Greenedge and its superstar Simon Gerrans, who became the first Australian to win Milan–San Remo (2012) and Liège–Bastogne–Liège (2014).

An extraordinary endurance cyclist, Opperman burst on the European scene in 1928 when he won the *Bol d'Or*, a paced 24-hour track event; after suffering several mechanicals, an ill-fitting bike and a dose of pure adrenalin-fuelled rage, Oppy made up a deficit of twenty laps and won the race, continuing on after the race to set a new 1000 kilometre record. He went on to take a creditable eighth at Paris–Rennes and an even better third in Paris–Brussels, then lined up at the same year's Tour de France, even though his Ravat-Wonder team only had four riders. Opperman described the experience as a 'nightmare' with stages begun in darkness and riders groping their way along mountain passes little better than goat tracks, without lights. Despite everything, Oppy would finish 18th on GC that year, and 12th three years later in 1931. He was voted 'most popular sportsman' in *l'Auto* in 1928, half a million French readers choosing him ahead of French tennis champion Henri Cochet. As popular with the media as the public, the *Petit Parisien* said of him 'Opperman's endurance, which is inversely proportional to his size and stature, brought him victory', while *Le journal* referred to him as 'a marvellous dynamo of human energy'.

Oppy went on to set a host of world records in endurance events, joined the Australian Air Force and became an Australian MP, eventually being knighted for his services as High Commissioner of Malta. In the spirit of a life well lived, you can ride the Hubert Opperman Gran Fondo or the Oppy Family Fun Ride – of which events it seems certain that Oppy, a lifelong cyclist who died on an exercise bike at the age of 91, would approve. But it was his insistence on his return to Australia after that 1928 Tour that Australia needed to introduce the French style of racing – freewheels, single tubes, air pumps, well-organised teams and knowledge of the race route – that has made Australia the formidable force in international cycling racing that it is today.

BLUFF FACT ► During the 1928 *Bol d'Or*, Oppy simply refused to leave the track to take a pee, so he let fly a long stream of urine that blew back into his opponents' faces, much to the crowd's delight.

P IS FOR ...

PELOTON

YOU SAY ► *PELL – A – TON (rhymes with yon)*

WHAT IT MEANS ► When the Tour de France made the decision to allow proper teams into the race in 1909, they inadvertently paved the way for a whole new cycling vocabulary. First up, how to describe a big group of riders working together? *Peloton* comes from an old French word meaning 'little ball' but it quickly became associated with a group of soldiers, or platoon. What better way to describe the regimented group of riders who take part in a cycle race? Michael Barry said of the experience of riding in the peloton: 'The peloton flows with the roads, and we, the cyclists, blindly hope that the flow is not broken. A wall of wheels and bodies means we can never see too far in front, so we trust that the peloton flows around any obstacle in the road like fish in a current.' When that flow is broken, the peloton tends to split into several groups – this can be as a result of weather conditions *(see E for Echelon)*, the demands of a climb *(see A for Autobus)* or obstacles in the road *(see C for Chute)*.

BLUFF FACT ► Each rider in the peloton makes an average of between 324,000 (at 60 rpm) and 486,000 (at 90 rpm) pedal strokes during a three week Grand Tour and the peloton wears out 792 tyres.

> **BLUFF IT** ► *'If you were to cycle 3,500km which is what the peloton cover during a Grand Tour you'd produce enough sweat to flush 39 toilets.'*

PACELINE

Otherwise known as a chain gang, learning to ride in a paceline is a basic skill as useful for a club ride as for the professional peloton. You can ride in a single or double paceline but the basic principle is the same – a rider takes their turn at the front of the line before dropping back to recover before moving through the paceline to take another turn at the front. In a single paceline it's just like a team pursuit *(see P)*. A double paceline is slightly more complicated: there are two lines, with one moving slightly more slowly than the other. The lead rider of the faster line moves sideways to the front of the slower line whilst the last rider in the slower line moves to the back of the faster line – imagine the way a bicycle chain moves around the gear cogs. The great thing about paceline riding is that it allows every rider to share the benefits of drafting *(see D)* which allows riders to save and recover energy when riding long distances.

PALMARÈS

YOU SAY ► *PAL – MAR (rhymes with tar) – REZ (rhymes with fez)*

WHAT IT MEANS ► Your *palmarès* are your achievements – your wins, podiums and top ten places. *Palmarès* comes from the Latin *palma* and it refers to the palm leaves that were once carried as a symbol of victory or success.

PANACHE

YOU SAY ▸ *P'NASH*

WHAT IT MEANS ▸ Ah, how to define the indefinable? For a 16th-century Italian, it would have been a flashy plume of feathers adorning his headgear. Edmond Rostand's play '*Cyrano de Bergerac*' popularised the idea of panache as a way of being – of courage and bravery in the face of defeat, where the way you fight the battle is more important than the winning or losing. The Oxford English Dictionary defines it as 'Flamboyant confidence of style or manner'. In cycling it's Thomas Voeckler defying Lance Armstrong in the Pyrenees to cling to the yellow jersey for a slender handful of seconds, or Claudio Chiappucci replicating the feat of his idol Fausto Coppi, riding 192 kilometres across the Croix de Fer, the Galibier and the Montgenèvre to win alone at Sestriere. It's in the handshake that the doomed breakaway companions share before they're swallowed by a speeding peloton, or in the faithful *domestique* who takes a well-deserved win at the back end of his career. It's in a sprint train hurtling under the *flamme rouge* at close to 70 km/h or a vertiginous descent as riders plummet from the heights of the tallest peaks. It plays directly into the romantic ideal that cycling has of itself, where a lone heroic rider can defy the might of the peloton to score a famous victory, or go down fighting in the attempt. The element of risk is crucial to panache – at any moment a rider may crash and burn and his effort come to nothing. So what is panache? Is it a rider playing to his strengths and smiting the opposition with a fatal blow where he is at his very strongest? Or a rider taking a huge gamble, win or lose, staking everything on one throw of the dice, one turn of the card, one massive, extraordinary attack?

PARACYCLING

Paracycling has been an Olympic sport since 1988 when eight road-cycling disciplines (for male riders only) were introduced at the Seoul Olympics. Track events were added eight years later with men and women competing. Other major competitions include the Paracycling World Championships and the Paracycling World Cup. Paracycling is fully integrated with other cycling disciplines and is governed by the UCI, who define the fourteen functional categories for men and women in the four handicaps: blind and visually impaired, cerebral palsy, locomotor disabilities and handcycling.

There are currently seven paracycling events for men and women: road race, time trial and handcycling relay (road events), and individual pursuit, 500 and 1km time trial, team sprint and tandem sprint (track events). There is a mixed event in the team sprint but the tandem sprint is currently a men-only event.

Prominent paracyclists include Dame Sarah Storey – Britain's most decorated Paralympian, she switched from the pool to the bike, enjoying equal success on the road and the track – and Alex Zanardi – the Italian racing car driver lost both his legs in an accident and is now a multiple medallist in the handcycling events.

PARCOURS

The French for the course of a race, this can refer to the route of a one-day race, a stage of a race or a stage race as a whole.

BLUFF IT ▸ *'I didn't think much of this year's Tour de France* parcours.*'*

PANTANI Marco

BORN ▸ 13 January, 1970, Cesena
(Emilia-Romagna), Italy
DIED ▸ 14 February, 2004, Rimini
(Emilia-Romagna), Italy
NATIONALITY ▸ Italian
RIDER TYPE ▸ Specialist climber, the finest of
his generation, perhaps of all time
ACTIVE ▸ 1992–2003
NICKNAMES ▸ Il Pirata (the Pirate), Diabolini
(Little Devil, after Claudio Chiappucci), Elefantino
and Dumbo (after his prominent ears – this was
the nickname Armstrong used after their duel on
Mont Ventoux – it sparked a lifelong feud between
the two riders)
BIG WINS ▸ 2 × young rider's jersey, Tour de France
(1994, 1995), Tour de France – Giro d'Italia double
(1998), king of the mountains, Giro d'Italia (1998)
MAJOR RIVAL ▸ Lance Armstrong

Marco Pantani's lonely death in a hotel room in Rimini in 2004 brought down the curtain on a career that had by turns soared to the very heights of the mountains he loved and descended into a kind of hell after his exclusion from the 1999 Giro d'Italia.

Success came quickly for the Italian, and a third and a second place at the Girobio in 1990 and 1991 led to his first professional contract the following year: at 22, he joined the famous Italian team, Carrera and steadily built an impressive series of results, finishing second in the Giro d'Italia and winning the white jersey for the best young rider at the 1994 Tour de France where he finished third. But he suffered two huge setbacks in 1995 – he was forced to abandon the Giro after a crash and was then involved in an accident at Milan–Turin that would have ended the career of many riders. He suffered multiple compound fractures to the left tibia and fibula after being hit head-on by a jeep. Nineteen months later, after a lengthy recuperation, he won on Alpe d'Huez for the first time, a climb for which he still holds the record.

But Pantani's career is best characterised in terms of his relationships with two of cycling's greatest riders – one the 'Angel of the Mountains', Charly Gaul; the other the great demon of the sport, Lance Armstrong.

With an angular physicality, Pantani possessed a birdlike quality that marks out the true and perfect climber. He became close friends with Gaul after the 1958 Tour winner – who had lived the life of a recluse in the Ardennes forest since his retirement from the sport in 1965 – expressed a desire to meet the Pirate after watching his performances in the 1994 Tour de France. Travelling to meet the Italian star in 1995, the two became close friends and Pantani even won one of the great Tour stages in 1998 *a la* 'Angel of the Mountains', attacking 50 kilometres from the finish on the ascent of the Galibier *(see G)* and riding through mist and rain to victory, much as Gaul had done in 1958 when he attacked on the Col de Luitel on his way to winning the Tour de France. The two were close in other ways. Almost identical in size and riding style, they were also similar in temperament, prone to mood swings that verged on paranoia yet with the steely determination to overcome what they often perceived as unfair and unjust. Gaul remained

CONTINUED OVERLEAF ▸

IL PIRATA

a friend to the end despite the accusations of doping that dogged the Italian's career after 1999 and was among the 20,000 mourners at Pantani's funeral in Censenatico. Gaul died in 2005, predeceased by his spiritual son and heir.

His enmity with Armstrong was born on the slopes of Mont Ventoux *(see V)* on 13 July, 2000, exactly 33 years after Tom Simpson's death on that infernal, bleached-out terrain. After an epic ascent, Armstrong claimed he had gifted the stage win to Pantani. The Italian was incensed, perceiving Armstrong's attitude as a humiliation. He took another stage win in the race – a superb solo win on the climb to Courchevel in the Alps where, gathering up all his rage and hatred and sense of injustice, he launched himself clear of Armstrong with five kilometres to the finish. Out of the saddle, he drove himself to the line for what would be his last ever professional win a full 51 seconds ahead of the American. He would never be on the start line of the race again.

Pantani would make veiled accusations against his adversary, casting doubt on the American's transformation from cancer survivor to all-conquering Tour de France hero. Though premonitory, those accusations might have applied to Pantani himself – retests of samples from the 1998 Tour de France showed that the Italian had used EPO during the race.

But the Pirate was already on the downward slope, a descent into hell that started on 5 June, 1999, when he was disqualified from the Giro d'Italia in Madonna di Campiglio for a haematocrit level of 52 per cent. Though withdrawal of a rider for a high haematocrit level (the cut-off had been set at 50 per cent by the UCI) was always referred to as a 'health measure', it was widely perceived as evidence of doping *(see D)*

– the higher the haematocrit, the higher the level of red blood cells in the blood. Pantani protested his innocence but the damage was done. And so began the decline into cocaine addiction and his long, lonely fight against 'the system'. What Lance Armstrong has experienced since his confession to Oprah Winfrey, Pantani lived through in the last five years of his life – the inescapable feeling that he had been scapegoated for the actions of a generation.

Scribbling his thoughts on the walls of his house, Panatani's innate fragility saw him crumble into depression and addiction.

So why is Pantani revered, where others like Virenque and Armstrong are reviled, where all are guilty of being part of that 'culture of champions'? There is a monument in his home town and stages in the Tour de France and the Giro have been dedicated to his memory. Part of it is the guilt that a champion could have been allowed to fall so far. Part is shock at the manner of his untimely and tragic death at 34. But there is also his legacy, frozen forever in photos and videos – the attacking, sublimely gifted pure *grimpeur (see G)* whose exploits in the highest mountains enthralled a generation of cycling fans and of whom the French sports paper *l'Équipe* once wrote 'Pantani embodied cycling. He *was* cycling.'

BLUFF FACT ▶ Pantani's Mercatone Uno team-mates had a bet with him in 1998 – if he won the Tour de France they'd dye their hair yellow. Pantani won and the team ended up with blonde hair.

> **BLUFF IT ▶** *'Pantani always got his weight down to the bare minimum before he attacked – he'd get rid of anything that might weigh him down, even his famous bandana and his earring.'*

PARIS–ROUBAIX

TYPE OF RACE ▸ One-day Classic

WHERE ▸ France

NICKNAMES ▸ The Hell of the North, Queen of the Classics

TERRAIN ▸ Flat with sectors of cobbles ranked in difficulty from one star (easy) to five star (insane)

TIME OF YEAR ▸ Spring, the Sunday after the Tour of Flanders

MULTIPLE WINS ▸ Roger de Vlaeminck and Tom Boonen have four wins apiece

MOST WINS BY COUNTRY ▸ Belgium, of course

GREAT MOMENTS ▸ Bernard Hinault winning by sheer force of will in the world champion's jersey in 1981 after multiple crashes and punctures; Coppi catching the breakaway, calmly pausing to eat an orange and then taking off alone for 100 kilometres to win in 1951 (of the two breakaway riders, one ended in the broom wagon and one retired a week later); Andrei Tchmil launching a brutal 62-kilometre attack to win solo in 1994; Johan Museeuw winning in 2000, two years after he had crashed in the Aarenberg and smashed his kneecap, almost losing his leg (he crossed the finish line alone, pointing at the scarred and battered kneecap as he did so); Steve Bauer's agonizing ten-minute wait in 1990 to find out that he'd lost by less than a centimetre to Eddy Planckaert in the tightest finish in the race's history; Roger Lapébie's disqualification in 1934 after he'd won the race on a spectator's bike (bike changes were forbidden); Tom Boonen's 2012 record-equalling win after a 56-kilometre solo attack.

They call it a Sunday in hell, and it's a race like no other. 'At other races we drink coffee, shake each other's hands, have a laugh,' says the Breton rider Guillaume Blot. 'But the morning of Paris–Roubaix no one speaks. It's war.' 2011 winner Johan Van Summeren says, 'If you're not scared, you're not ready. You need all your wits about you.' Theo de Rooij said it best: 'It's a shitty race! We ride like animals, we don't even have the time to take a piss so we piss in our shorts – it's a pile of shit.' But would he come back and ride again? 'Of course, it's the most beautiful race in the world!'

The 27 sectors of dusty, rugged *pavé* – the sections of old, battered cobblestones that characterise the race – are graded in difficulty from the one-starred Templeuve l'Épinette to the five-star brutality of the Carrefour de l'Arbre and the Trouée Arenberg, a long treacherous cobbled trench through a foreboding forest. These are not the smooth, rounded, regular cobbles of the Tour of Flanders but rough-hewn lumps of granite that give the race its unique character.

For shaking his bones and joints and internal organs across the cobbles; for driving his body and bike for close to six hours through that inhospitable, windblown landscape; for jumping and jarring every fibre until he wants to puke with fatigue; for finally entering the concrete banking of the iconic velodrome and sprinting for the win like a fresh legged track rider not a heavy legged road warrior – for this the winner receives €30,000 and a cobblestone that is beyond price. Supplied by a family of masons in Orchies, that simple lump of granite is the Jules Rimet trophy of cycling. When Andrea Tafi finally took a famous, sentimental victory in 1999 he let the organisers know he wanted to use his *pavé* as the keystone of his new house. Obligingly, they provided another for his trophy cabinet.

Last stop for those who manage to stay the course in the Queen of the Classics – the Roubaix velodrome showers. As the grime and pain of a day in the hell of the north sluices away down the drain, each rider will find himself reflecting on disappointment or triumph in those simple open concrete cubicles, shoulder height, each bearing a brass plaque with the name of a previous winner. They are the final stop on the hellish road that leads from Compiègne to Roubaix. 'When I stand in the showers in Roubaix,' Tom Boonen said in 2004, after finishing ninth behind Magnus Backstedt, 'I actually start the preparation for next year.' True to his word, Boonen scored his first win a year later.

BLUFF IT ► *'The cobbled sectors are looked after by the* Amis de Paris–Roubaix *– thanks to them the race continues on roads first laid down in Napoleonic times.'*

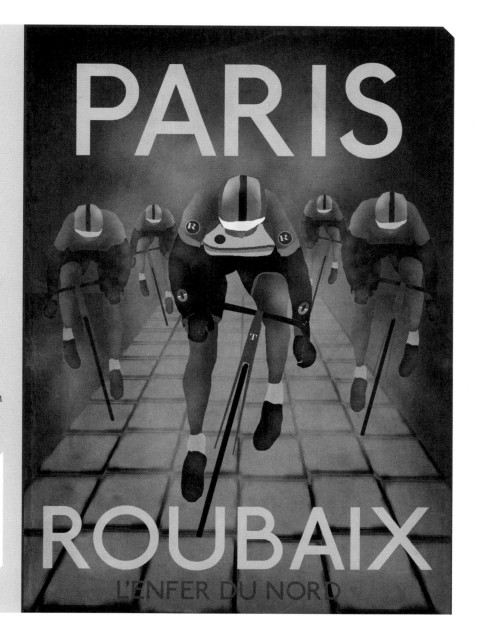

PARIS

ROUBAIX

L'ENFER DU NORD

PATRON

YOU SAY ► *PAT – RON*

WHAT IT MEANS ► Other sports may have their dominant figures, their huge stars, but in no other sport will you find a *patron*. He is the boss of the peloton – the rider who decides who can attack and when, who negotiates with the race organisers and who stands up for the rights of the riders. Bernard Hinault once famously declared 'there will be no attacks today because tomorrow's stage will be difficult' and would aggressively ride down riders who disobeyed his diktats. The *patron* exerts overall control of the race and demands – and receives – respect. Riders like Fabian Cancellara and Bradley Wiggins have acted as *le patron* in ordering the peloton to neutralise stages in the Tour de France. But not every yellow jersey wants the responsibility of exerting the authority that comes with the job of *patron*, some are content simply to get on with the job of winning.

PAVÉ

YOU SAY ► *PAV (as in pavlova) – VAY (rhymes with way)*

WHAT IT MEANS ► *Pavé* is the French for cobblestone. Cobbles give the Tour of Flanders and Paris–Roubaix their special character, shaking and rattling the rider's bones for over 200 kilometres. Whereas the cobbles of Flanders tend to be smaller, smoother and more evenly laid, those of Paris–Roubaix are larger, rougher and more elemental – laid on sand, they move under your feet or wheels and look as if they've been dropped from a helicopter and patted in place by a giant child with a spade. And they're treacherous – a skating rink when wet, they're a string of potholes when dry. The specialists agree that the best place to be on the cobbles is right on the spine of the road – it's easier

to ride in the gutter but that's where the potholes and sharp stones lie in wait to cause a puncture. The best rules for riding the *pavé* are: keep your tyre pressure low, relax your body (no clutching the handlebars in a death grip) and enjoy. And the faster you go, the quicker they'll be over!

BLUFF FACT ► The cobbles in the Tour of Flanders are nicknamed kinderkoppen or 'babys' heads'.

PEDAL

The pedal connects to the crank which connects to the chainring which drives the rear wheel. Apply pressure to the pedal with your foot and off you go. A fluent pedal stroke is much admired and improves your efficiency – the French even have a word for it, *souplesse* (literally, suppleness or flexibility), and it's the difference between appearing to stomp on the pedals with great effort and being able to spin effortlessly with maximum efficiency.

One of the greatest exponents of *souplesse* was Hugo Koblet, the Swiss rider, whose beautiful style earned him the nickname '*Pedaleur de Charme*'. In one of the great Tour de France exploits *(see E)*, Koblet attacked on a seemingly innocuous stage between Brive and Agen in the 1951 Tour de France – with 135 kilometres to the finish line, the Swiss simply pulled clear of the opposition and, with metronomic efficiency, maintained at least a two-minute gap all the way to victory. When you consider that the group chasing him contained Fausto Coppi *(see C)*, Louison Bobet (first man to win the Tour three times in a row), Gino Bartali *(see B)*, Fiorenzo Magni (winner of the Giro in 1948, 1951 and 1955), Raphaël Géminiani (who was the king of the mountains in the Tour and the Giro in 1951), Stan Ockers (who won the Tour de France green points jersey in

CONTINUED OVERLEAF ►

1955 and 1956) and Jean Robic (winner of the 1947 Tour), it was an even more extraordinary achievement. But Koblet saved the *coup de grâce* for the finish line – he took a small damp sponge from his jersey pocket and washed his handsome face, combed his abundant hair and then calmly dismounted and set his stopwatch running ... What a *pedaleur*! What *charme*!

BLUFF FACT ▶ Koblet also suffered terribly with haemorrhoids and had been on the point of abandoning the race the night before until he found a doctor who prescribed him a cream with a little extra ingredient – cocaine. No wonder the Swiss flew all the way to the finish ...

PEDALLING SQUARES

When a rider is exhausted and can no longer push the pedals round with ease they are said to be 'pedalling squares' instead of smooth circles. Imagine that the cranks are going round in a square and you'll have an idea of just what hard work a rider is putting in just to keep going. Most often seen in mountain stages when the gradient is at its steepest.

PENDLETON Victoria

BORN ▶ 24 September, 1980, Stotfold (Bedfordshire), UK
NATIONALITY ▶ British
ACTIVE ▶ 1999–2012
RIDER TYPE ▶ Track sprint specialist
NICKNAME ▶ Queen Victoria
BIG WINS ▶ 2 × Olympic gold (2008, 2012), 9 × world champion (2005, 2007, 2008, 2009, 2010, 2012), 2 × European champion (2011), 1 × Commonwealth gold (2006)
MAJOR RIVAL ▶ Anna Meares

Victoria Pendleton is Britain's most successful ever female Olympian, winning two golds and a silver in Beijing and London. A pure track sprinter, she dominated the sprint and keirin disciplines for eight years and was world sprint champion for three years in a row out of a total six world sprint titles. Talent spotted at the age of 16, after excelling in grass-track sprint races, Pendleton chose education over training but, inspired by Jason Queally's Olympic success she began to train in earnest and spent two seasons at the World Cycling Centre in Aigle, Switzerland. She was one of the great success stories of the British Cycling funding boom and made history in 2007 when she won an unprecedented three world titles in Mallorca, taking the sprint, team sprint and keirin.

But her career was defined by her rivalry with Anna Meares. Both five foot five inches tall, Pendleton epitomises slender elegance on a bike as opposed to the pugnacious, stocky Australian. Pendleton characterised her adversary as someone who liked to 'push the rules' and their head to head meetings enthralled spectators around the world. From Athens in 2004 to London in 2012, they traded blows in the sprint and keirin disciplines like two heavyweight boxers. Their contests were never tighter than at the world championships in Melbourne, Australia where the two riders met in the sprint semi-finals. Pendleton tangled with Meares in the first heat and ended on the boards. In the second heat, Meares was disqualified for going outside her line. In the third, Pendleton edged it in the tightest of photo finishes. It was the Briton who would go on to win her ninth – and final – world title. Her last appearance in the velodrome at the London 2012 Olympics saw her imperious in winning the keirin, but she lost out to Meares in the sprint and made her tearful and emotional farewell to the competitive sport.

Pendleton retired from cycling in 2012. She holds a BSc (hons) in Sports and Exercise Science, was awarded an honorary doctorate of Civil Law and is a CBE for services to cycling. She has also co-authored a book about her life in cycling and designed her own range of bicycles. She used her gold medal winning legs to samba, waltz and cha cha on the BBC dance competition 'Strictly Come Dancing'. Pendleton has not one, but two, gold postboxes dedicated to her Olympic achievements.

> **BLUFF IT** ▶ *'For her 30th birthday, she had "today is the greatest day I've ever known" – from a Smashing Pumpkins song – tattooed on her arm.'*

PODIUM

The podium is the stage on which the jersey presentations are made after a race. Can also refer to the riders who finish first, second and third in a race as in 'the podium saw X beat Y with Z rounding out the podium places.'

PODIUM GIRLS

The podium girl is either a way of feminising what is otherwise an almost completely male bastion of sport or a sexist anachronism in the 21st century. Podium girls – or hostesses as they are supposed to be known – have the responsibility not just of giving the day's winners their jerseys and a kiss on the cheek but also providing hospitality to sponsors and VIPs, hosting parties and a range of other public relations roles. Required to be on duty, perfectly groomed and with a ready smile, from morning to night (and to drive a car up a mountain if asked) the podium girl helps to oil the wheels of cycling's biggest events.

Once chosen from the female populace of towns where a race would finish, with the only requirements being that they were under 30 and didn't dwarf the (usually diminutive) riders, podium girls are now chosen as much for their endurance, personality and language skills as for their looks alone. Some put themselves forward but most are proposed by modelling agencies and will have some experience of event organisation. From around 500 hopefuls, only four are eventually chosen to do the most prestigious job of all – presenting the yellow jersey. And all for the joy of getting your bum pinched by Peter Sagan, as happened to Maja Leye on the podium of the 2013 Tour of Flanders (the Slovakian rider was quick to apologise).

BLUFF FACT ► Fraternising with riders is strictly a no-go area, but it didn't stop Melanie Simonneau from choosing George Hincapie over her career as a podium girl in 2003. After exchanging text messages throughout the race, the rider and the hostess married and now have two children: 'I basically pursued her around France,' admitted the American rider.

> **BLUFF IT** ► *'The women's race La Course has podium boys which either legitimises the whole outmoded concept or is a stroke of utter genius.'*

POURSUIVANT

YOU SAY ► *POUR – SWEE – VON*
WHAT IT MEANS ► The *poursuivant* – or *inseguitore* in Italian, *achtervolger* (literally back follower) in Dutch, *perseguidor* in Spanish – is the rider (or riders) chasing – pursuing – the leaders of the race.

PROLOGUE

The prologue is a short individual time trial – no longer than eight kilometres – that opens a stage race. It's an opportunity for the real specialists to show what they can do and for the general classification riders to steal a few seconds over their rivals – or try not to lose too much time if they're mountain goats.

PUNCHEUR

YOU SAY ► *PUNCH – UR (to rhyme with fur)*
WHAT IT MEANS ► Exactly as he sounds, the *puncheur* is a punchy rider, specialising in rolling terrain with short, steep climbs. He can accelerate away in the one-day Classics but doesn't have the stamina for the longer climbs of the high mountains.

PURSUIT

It's quite simple: two riders – or teams – start at opposite sides of the track and ride as fast as their legs can pedal to record the quickest time over 4000 metres (the UCI equalised the distances for men and women in 2014). Staying low on the pursuit line to maximise their speed, the ultimate goal is to catch the other rider or team. If the catch is made, the pursuit is over – but riders often choose to keep going for the full distance in order to record a fast qualification time, or attempt to break a record in the final. Qualification is done on time, with the two fastest individuals or teams riding off against each other in the final.

Where the individual pursuit is all about pure speed, the team pursuit adds the element of beautifully coordinated team work. The better the four riders work together and the more slickly they change position in the team formation, the quicker their time. It works like this: the first rider, the lead-out man, rides on the front for the first lap and a quarter as fast as possible. When he tires, he rides up the banking of the bend of the velodrome – that's the slope of the track – so that the second rider can take his place, with the first rider slotting into fourth place. The four riders repeat this chain effect, rising and falling off the banking, over the 16 laps of the

pursuit. The team's time is taken when the front wheel of the third rider crosses the finish line so it's quite common to see a rider put in a huge effort over the last kilometre before dropping off the pace as his team-mates speed towards the line. It's beautiful to watch and, when done with great discipline and control, can see riders touching speeds of 64 km/h.

Once part of the Olympic cycling programme, the individual pursuit was removed from the Olympics in 2012 but continues to be part of the omnium *(see O)*. But you can still become world pursuit champion as an individual or a team.

Q IS FOR ...

QUEEN STAGE

From the French *étape reine*, in Italian *il tappone*. This is the big mountain stage in any stage race – the one that contains the highest peaks and the most difficult climbs. Usually intended as the hardest stage in the race, things don't always turn out that way – crashes and other incidents can make the most seemingly innocuous of stages into game changers, while a stage that on paper has a profile like shark's teeth can turn out to be a total damp squib if the favourites decide not to race each other that day.

QUICK RELEASE

The quick-release skewer is a mechanism that allows a rider – or mechanic – to remove and replace a wheel quickly and easily.

The story goes that Tullio Campagnolo – founder of the renowned bicycle component company of the same name – was competing in the 1924 edition of the Gran Premio della Vittoria road race. Needing to make a gear change on the fearsome climb of the Croce d'Aune in the Dolomites, Campagnolo was forced to dismount and remove his rear wheel *(see D for Derailleur for more on this process)* in a snowstorm. Fumbling with frozen fingers at the wing nuts that held the wheel in place and unable to remove them quickly and easily, Campagnolo – who was losing valuable time – is supposed to have said '*Bisogna cambiar qualcossa de drio*' – 'something needs changing at the back'. So he set about changing it, patenting the prototype quick-release skewer – now standard on performance racing bikes – in the early 1930s.

RIDER

QUINTANA Nairo

BORN ▸ 4 February, 1990, Tunja (Boyacá), Colombia
NATIONALITY ▸ Colombian
ACTIVE ▸ 2009–
RIDER TYPE ▸ All-rounder/climbing specialist
NICKNAMES ▸ Italian sport's paper *La Gazzetta dello Sport* have dubbed him 'El Condor', a favourite for Colombian riders; also El Negro (an affectionate term in Colombia) and Naironman. But he is most likely to be simply 'Nairo' as Luis 'Lucho' Herrera was simply 'Lucho'
BIG WINS ▸ Giro d'Italia overall and best young rider (2014), king of the mountains and best young rider, Tour de France (2013), Tour de l'Avenir (2010)
MAJOR RIVALS ▸ Chris Froome, Alberto Contador

Nairo Quintana announced himself on the world scene at the age of 20 when he won the *Tour de l'Avenir* (Tour of the Future), a French race designed to discover the grand-tour riders of the future. Past winners have included three-time Tour de France winner America's Greg LeMond *(see L)* and his twice Tour winning rival, Frenchman Laurent Fignon.

Quintana grew up in abject poverty, but his parents scraped together the money to buy him a second-hand mountain bike so he was able to cycle the 16 kilometres to school. Since joining the Spanish Movistar team in 2012, the Colombian's career has exploded with wins in several smaller stage races including the Route du Sud (2012) and the Tour of the Basque Country (2013) and the white jersey of best young rider and the polka dot jersey of the king of the mountains at his debut

Tour de France plus second place overall behind Chris Froome *(see F)*. But it was Quintana's victory at the 2014 Giro d'Italia – his first participation in the race – that announced him as a major talent and bought Colombian cycling back to the forefront of cycling fans' attention.

Quintana is not the first Colombian to win a Grand Tour *(see G)* – that was Luis Herrera who won the Vuelta a España in 1987, when Colombian riders first appeared on the international scene. But the Colombian riders, who made their debut at the 1983 Tour de France as an amateur team, never capitalised on their extraordinary climbing abilities – as Robert Millar *(see M)* said, if there was a crash in the race you'd generally find a Colombian at the bottom of it. Herrera did win on the Alpe d'Huez *(see A)* in 1984 but it is the new generation of riders like Quintana, Rigoberto Urán and Carlos Betancur who are finally proving that South American riders have the complete skill set to win the biggest prizes in cycling.

In August 2013, the Colombian president honoured Quintana with the 'Order of Boyacá, Commanders level' for his achievements in the 2013 Tour de France. Usually bestowed as a military decoration, the Order of Boyacá can also be given to Colombian citizens who have achieved the extraordinary.

BLUFF IT ▸ *'Quintana's childhood home was up an eight per cent climb – instead of getting the polka dot jersey his parents would wrap him up in a ruana (a Colombian poncho – Boyacá is known for its chilly temperatures).'*

R IS FOR...

R IS FOR ...

RAINBOW STRIPES

Every rider dreams that one day he'll wear the rainbow jersey of the world champion and earn the right to wear the distinctive striped jersey for a year. The world road race champion earns the right to wear his rainbow striped jersey in any race he enters, unless he earns a leader's jersey. The world time-trial champion may only wear their stripes when competing against the clock. But a world champion earns the right to wear the rainbow stripes ever afterwards at the neck and cuffs of his team jersey. Some riders have had a disastrous season after winning the world championship, leading to the idea of the 'curse of the rainbow jersey', but it didn't befall Eddy Merckx, Bernard Hinault or Greg LeMond who all won the Tour de France in the rainbow stripes.

ROAD FURNITURE

The speed bumps and concrete road islands, cat's eyes and traffic lights, bollards and central reservations that clutter European roads are known as road furniture and can be defined as any changes to the road surface designed to change driving speeds. Road furniture can cause havoc in a cycle race as it disrupts the consistency of the road surface that cyclists rely on. For larger races like the Classics and the Grand Tours, obstacles like speed bumps will be removed and replaced, but there's no doubt that the increase in traffic-calming measures has made cycle racing more dangerous for riders and spectators alike. In the 2014 Amstel Gold Race, Johan Vansummeren crashed straight into a small traffic island and hit a spectator. Both the rider and a spectator ended up in hospital.

BLUFF IT ▸ *'Road furniture is that stuff in the middle of the road that doesn't move and hurts like hell when you hit it!'*

ROCHE Stephen

BORN ▸ 28 November, 1959, Dublin (Leinster), Republic of Ireland

NATIONALITY ▸ Irish

ACTIVE ▸ 1981–1993

RIDER TYPE ▸ All-rounder, aggressive in the mountains and strong against the clock

NICKNAME ▸ 'Beryl Burton' (an in-joke, supposedly for his youthful head of curls that resembled the great British woman rider's)

BIG WINS ▸ Giro d'Italia (1987), Tour de France (1987), world road race champion (1987), 3 × Tour of Romandie (1983, 1984, 1987)

MAJOR RIVALS ▸ Pedro Delgado

Ireland's Stephen Roche is the only other rider beside Eddy Merckx *(see M)* to have achieved cycling's triple crown – winning the Giro, Tour and worlds in the same year. Roche also won the prestigious year-long Super Prestige Pernod competition in his *annus mirabilis* 1987.

Announcing himself on the professional scene with a first time victory against Bernard Hinault *(see H)*, the Irishman went on to win Paris–Nice in 1981 as a neo-pro (first-year professional), the only time this feat has been achieved.

But it is for his miraculous 1987 season that Roche deserves his place in the record books. Despite a serious knee injury sustained in a crash on the track that wiped out his 1986 season and saw him finish one hour 32 minutes behind Greg LeMond in the Tour de France, Roche arrived on the startline in France the following year with a victory at the Giro d'Italia already under his belt.

The Irishman had won three of the five time trials in that race and, against team orders, attacked his team-mate Roberto Visentini, the 1986 Giro winner, earning the hatred of the Italian *tifosi (see T)*. That day in the Dolomites earned the nickname the 'Marmolada Massacre' *(see M)*.

But it is stage 21 in the 1987 Tour de France, the 185 kilometres between Bourg d'Oisans and La Plagne, that has come to define Roche's career. Having poached the yellow jersey on stage 19 with an opportunistic attack on French leader Jean-François Bernard at the feed zone, Roche promptly lost it the next day to Spain's Pedro Delgado on the Alpe d'Huez *(see A)*. And it was Delgado who had the Irishman on the ropes again on the final climb to La Plagne, gaining a one minute 15 seconds advantage on the ascent. But he reckoned without Roche's determination to win. Gambling on riding at his own pace and limiting his losses, then going flat out over the final four kilometres, Roche later recalled that desperate effort to keep himself in contention: 'I was good on the tactical and psychological side and I just went for it. If I'd had the kind of info they get on the Tour today I might have eased off when I was just 30 seconds down on Delgado. But because I thought the gap was so much bigger I kept grinding on. I was in survival mode. I didn't even register what I'd done.' What he'd done was to finish just seconds down on the Spaniard and haul himself back to just 39 seconds behind Delgado on GC *(see G)*, but no one could quite believe that it was Roche who had crossed the line just behind the Spaniard – journalists were forced to rewrite their stories and Phil Liggett (the English-speaking commentator) had to re-record his commentary. But his immortal line 'Who's that rider coming up behind – it looks like Roche – that looks like Stephen Roche – IT'S STEPHEN ROCHE!!!' added to what has become one of the most iconic of all Tour de France stages. The day that Stephen Roche saved the Tour de France. He would pull on the yellow jersey on the penultimate stage of the race, a 38-kilometre time trial, where he finished one minute and one second ahead of Delgado. With only the procession into Paris, the yellow jersey was his to keep.

The Dubliner finished the year by winning the world road race championships in Austria, assuring his place in cycling history. Though he achieved further stage wins at the Tour de France and would win the Tour of the Basque Country in 1989, his world champion season saw the 'curse of the rainbow jersey' *(see R)* strike – the old knee injury flared up again – and his career went into decline. There were rumours of doping at his Carrera team, who were ruled to have used EPO in 1993. But that one extraordinary, torrid day in the French Alps, and the titanic effort Roche made to keep his dreams of yellow alive, make stage 21 in the 1987 Tour one of the greatest moments in the race's history.

BLUFF FACT ► Roche was so depleted by his effort that he needed oxygen after collapsing off his bike. When French reporters asked him how he was feeling he replied 'Everything's okay, *mais pas de femme ce soir*' (but no women tonight).

ROAD RASH

You know when you crash, badly, and leave little bits of your skin all over the tarmac? What the road gives you in return – those bloody red abrasions that make you feel somehow like you're doing this for real – that's road rash. The cyclist's badge of honour.

ROLLERS

You'll see professional cyclists warming up and cooling down on these before and after a time trial. An indoor training device, it comprises a set of cyclinders that roll when you place your bike on them and pedal in place. Also useful for training when the weather is particularly miserable or you're coming back from an injury.

ROULEUR

YOU SAY ► *ROO – LUR (rhymes with fur)*
WHAT IS IT? ► These are the riders who can turn a huge gear with seeming effortless ease for kilometre after kilometre across the flat lands of the cycling landscape. Usually larger riders who provide a useful windbreak, they typically excel at efforts against the clock – the Swiss rider Fabian Cancellara is a *rouleur par excellence* equally capable of sheltering his team leader or of putting in a devastating solo effort to win a time trial or a Classic. Between them Cancellara and his Belgian counterpart Tom Boonen have won six of the last ten Tours of Flanders and seven of the last ten Paris–Roubaix, the ideal one-day races for the *rouleurs*.

S IS FOR ...

SPRINT/SPRINTER

There are two kinds of sprinting – track and road – both equally fast and furious and the most exciting thing you can watch on two wheels. The fastest of the fast, the real speed demons of the sport are the sprinters. Far heavier than the skinny little mountain goats, a sprinter's power lies in the combination of powerful thigh muscles, upper body strength and the all-important fast-twitch muscle fibre that contracts quickly and is ideal for short, sharp efforts.

Most road sprinters rely on their leadout train *(see L)*: a dedicated 'team within the team' that delivers their sprinter to the line in optimum condition to contest the win. The leadout train was the invention of the Panasonic team in the 1980s, but it was Mario Cipollini's Saeco team that elevated it to an art form – the 'red train' delivered 122 victories for their sprinter. Each rider in the train takes their turn to ride as hard as possible on the front, before peeling off to let their teammate take up the work. Eventually, the main leadout man – or *poisson pilote* (pilot fish) – delivers his sprinter the last 100 metres to the line. A road sprint may look chaotic as the sprinters hurtle to the finish, but there are strict rules about staying on your line. If riders are seen to veer across the road or inhibit other riders, they face disqualification and will usually be placed last in the results for the stage or race. The so called 'Abdoujaparov Rule' is named after the sprinter from Tashkent who was notorious for hurtling his bike around in the sprint in the 1990s. And let's face it, a bunch sprint is a dangerous enough place to be without reckless riding.

Track sprinting is a totally different affair, pitting man against man on the boards of the velodrome. This is the

CONTINUED OVERLEAF ▶

very essence of sprinting, with a set of rules that can seem arcane and mysterious and tactics that can be baffling. So let's take it lap by lap – remember, this is a 750-metre race where only the last 200 metres count.

Lap one: usually taken at a snail's pace it may even involve the riders coming to a total standstill without putting their feet down on the boards – this is the track stand, a useful skill for any commuter stuck at a red light. It's also the lap where the riders suss each other out, probing for weaknesses and trying to force each other to take the lead position.

Lap two: this lap sees the riders winding up speed for the big finish and attempting to take possession of the track underneath the 'sprinter's line' which is marked 80cm from the base of the track. This is the place every sprinter wants to be inside the final 200m as your rival is forced to come around your outside. Most disqualifications come about because a rider tries to muscle their opponent out of this all-important position by trying to come past them on the inside. It's on this lap that you often see the sprinters force each other up onto the banking, the sloping sides of the velodrome, all the better to dive down and seize the advantage.

Lap three: this is the charge for the line and the sprint for glory. Match sprinting is usually best of three – if you can't get past your opponent, you're better off saving your energy for the next round.

The team sprint – sometimes known as the Olympic Sprint – doesn't really resemble a sprint in the conventional sense. Contested by three-man or two-woman teams who start on opposite sides of the track, each member of the team rides one lap before leaving the track to let their speediest rider record the quickest possible time over the final lap.

SADDLE

This is the bit you sit on and it serves exactly the same purpose as a horse saddle: to spread your weight and act as one of the three points of contact between the rider and the bike (the other two are the handlebars and the pedals). The original draisine – the prototype for all bikes, often known as the hobby horse and not unlike a child's balance bike – had no seat at all. As the bicycle developed the seat could be as simple as a plank of wood or as relatively complicated as a ring of metal. It wasn't until the development of the safety bicycle that the need for a comfortable saddle was considered. Legend has it that John Brooks, whose father was a saddler, experimented with covering a wooden bicycle saddle with leather in 1865. The modern saddle is generally a hard shell, often plastic, covered with a thin layer of padding and a cover of fabric or leather.

SADDLE SORES

A pain in the arse – quite literally – caused by pressure on the sitting bones, friction or, worst of all, a furuncle (aka a good old fashioned boil on the butt). A good chamois cream (a moisturiser applied before getting your lycra shorts on) is a must.

BLUFF FACT ▶ Sean Kelly *(see K)*, who was leading the race at the time, had to retire from the 1987 Vuelta a España because of a saddle sore, just three days from the finish in Madrid.

SERVICE COURSE

YOU SAY ► *SIR – VEESE (rhymes with peace) COURSE*

WHAT IT IS ► A French term, *service course* (which translates as race assistance) is the storage facility of any cycling team where bikes and all related gear – from inner tubes to power bars – are stored and maintained. Depending on budget that can be a van or a warehouse.

Service course also refers to the yellow neutral service cars provided by Mavic in the Tour de France, whose job is to offer mechanical assistance to a rider if their team car can't get through the other support cars to help them out.

SOIGNEUR

YOU SAY ► *SWAN – YER (to rhyme with her)*

WHAT IT MEANS ► *Soigneur* comes from the French verb *soigner* – to care, to look after, to nurse or to treat, and all of these are essential to the *soigneur's* role. In a typical day s/he might be expected to prepare the *bidons (see B)* and *musettes (see M)* for the team and hand them out at the feed zone, make sandwiches for the support staff, tote luggage to and from the team hotel, provide riders with drinks and warm clothing at the finish line, make sure the riders are protected from intrusive media, collect and wash the dirty laundry, give massage therapy – and then repeat, day in day out, during the length of the season that runs from the Tour Down Under in Australia in January to the Tour of Beijing in China in October. There has been a darker side to the role of *soigneur*: for much of the 20th century they also looked after a rider's medical needs which inevitably tipped over into quackery – with *soigneurs* recommending their riders consume everything from cattle feed to carrot juice – and doping, with *soigneurs* procuring, transporting and administering performance-enhancing products. The nadir came when Willy Voet, a *soigneur* for the Festina team, had his car stopped and searched on the way to the 1998 Tour de France. He was carrying a cargo of EPO. Voet went to prison and the sport was finally forced to start cleaning up its act.

> **BLUFF IT ►** *'Just off to get a rub down from my swanny.' (Swanny is English slang for a* soigneur.)

STAGE

Otherwise known as *étape (see E)* – one of the one-day races that make up a cycling stage race. In Italian races it's a *tappa* and in Spain riders set off to ride an *etapa*.

> **BLUFF IT ►** *When Henri Desgrange and Geo Lefevre came up with the idea for a bicycle Tour de France they invented the new sport of stage racing.*

SIMPSON Tom

BORN ▸ 30 November, 1937, Haswell (County Durham), England
DIED ▸ 13 July, 1967, Mont Ventoux (Provence), France
NATIONALITY ▸ British
ACTIVE ▸ 1959–1967
RIDING STYLE ▸ All-rounder
NICKNAMES ▸ Major Tom, Mr Tom
BIG WINS ▸ Tour of Flanders (1961), Milan–San Remo (1964), Giro di Lombardia (1965), world road race champion (1965), Paris–Nice (1967)
MAJOR RIVALS ▸ Jan Janssen, Roger Pingeon

Tom Simpson was the first British rider to win a Monument *(see M)*, the first British winner of Milan–San Remo and still the only British winner of the Tour of Flanders and the Giro di Lombardia. And he was the first Briton to pull on that most iconic of all jerseys, the *maillot jaune* of the leader of the Tour de France.

Born in the north-east of England, the son of a coalminer, after a successful amateur career Simpson moved to Brittany, France in 1959. Professional success quickly followed with the Briton winning a hard fought finish in the Tour of Flanders in 1961 – the wind was so strong the banner for the finish line blew down – and took the yellow jersey in the Tour de France (then lost it the next day) in 1962. His world championships win at San Sebastián in Spain in 1965 was

classic Simpson: attacking with two laps to go on a hilly circuit, he stayed clear with only Germany's Rudi Altig (with whom he'd ridden a two-man time trial event the year before) for company. Simpson was given to long solo attacks to compensate for his relatively poor sprint, but this time his luck held – sprinting as hard as he could for the line, he won the race just as his bike tyre was about to explode.

After breaking his leg in a skiing accident, Simpson's 1966 season was a washout, but he was back for the 1967 season and ready for the Tour. At 29, he knew his time was running out to cash in on his success and make enough money to retire – a strong performance in France would guarantee the lucrative post-race criterium (town-centre circuit races, whose result was fixed in advance) contracts that many riders relied on to supplement their wages. Félix Lévitan decided that the 1967 Tour de France would be contested by national teams for the first time since 1961. This immediately put Simpson at a disadvantage with an understrength British team and it was his teammate at Peugeot, Frenchman Roger Pingeon, who would come out of retirement to win the race.

But the name Tom Simpson is inextricably wedded to what happened on stage 13, the 211.5-kilometre ride between Marseille and Carpentras with its passage over the summit of Mont Ventoux *(see V)* of which Simpson had written 'it's like another world up there among the bare rocks and the glaring sun.' The stage was set for July 13, 1967. What happened next was the collision between ambition and desperation with one man caught in a perfect storm of heat, dehydration, amphetamines and alcohol. As the race left the shade of the tree line

and headed for the molten, barren landscape of lunar rock Simpson started to zig and zag across the road 'the way amateurs do when they're in trouble,' said his mechanic, Harry Hall. When Simpson collapsed, Hall tried to persuade him to abandon but the Briton insisted on riding on, only to collapse again shortly afterwards. Despite the best efforts of the race doctor, Dr Pierre Dumas, who had successfully saved the life of French rider Jean Malléjac in an almost identical incident in 1955, Simpson could not be saved. He died by the roadside a few kilometres from the summit, the spot marked by a memorial paid for by a British cyclist for whom Simpson's achievements far outweighed the manner of his death.

Simpson's team-mate Eddy Merckx was at his funeral in Harworth, near Doncaster and would pay his respects at the Simpson memorial when he won a stage on the Ventoux on his way to winning the 1970 Tour de France. A plaque was added on the thirtieth anniversary of his death by his daughters, Jane and Joanne, which simply reads, 'There is no mountain too high.'

BLUFF FACT ▶ Simpson's oft quoted last words 'put me back on my bike' were actually invented by a British reporter for 'Cycling' magazine, Sid Saltmarsh.

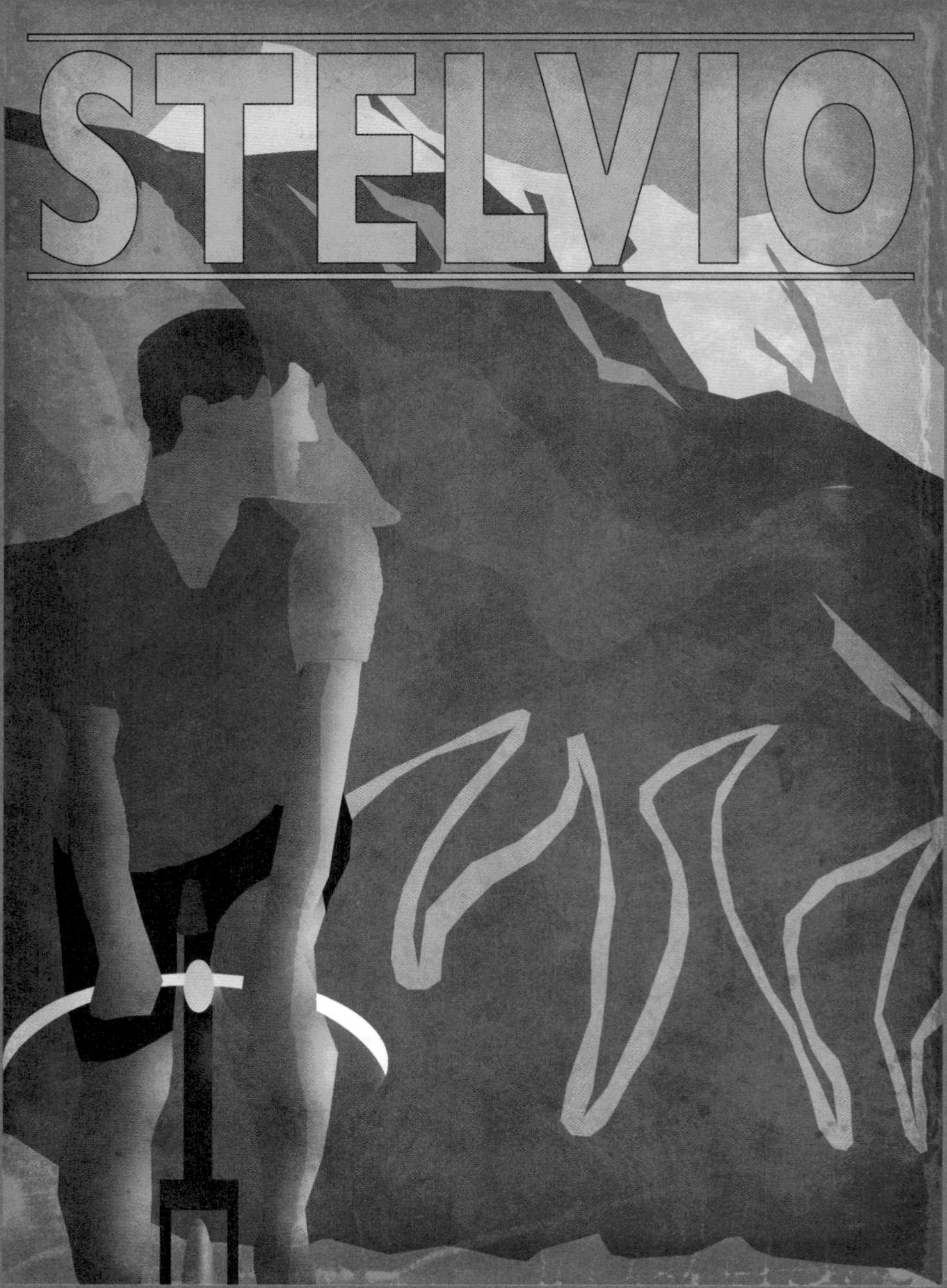
STELVIO

STELVIO

ALTITUDE ▶ 2758 metres
HEIGHT GAIN ▶ 1808 metres
AVERAGE GRADIENT ▶ 7.4 per cent
MAXIMUM GRADIENT ▶ 12.1 per cent
LENGTH ▶ 24.3 kilometres
LOCATION ▶ Italian Alps

The Giro d'Italia loves its mountains and none more so than the Stelvio, whose 48 hairpins – more than twice those of the Alpe d'Huez in France – wind up one of the highest mountain passes in Europe. Fausto Coppi was the first man to win here in 1953, when he seized the pink jersey in a ferocious attack on then unpaved roads, to win his fifth and final Giro. The *cima Coppi* – the prize awarded to the rider who is first to cross the highest pass in the Giro d'Italia – is sometimes awarded here, though the mountain is often still impassable in May because of the snow that clings to its barren peak. Even when the race makes it to the summit, the riders often pass between the walls of snow and ice, the road having been cleared only days before. The Stelvio reserves its biggest test for its final kilometres where the gradient ramps up to a maximum 12.1 per cent and its twists and turns are at their most dangerous and tortuous but the descent is more terrifying. British cyclist Brian Smith described it as 'the most horrible descent I've ever done … I was petrified'.

STICKY BOTTLE

Like the 'magic spanner' *(see M)* the sticky bottle is the one that is handed from the team car and never quite seems to leave one hand or arrive in another, allowing a rider to take a breather and a not-so-sneaky tow from the team car. Particularly useful on long mountain stages.

STRADA Alfonsina

The 'Devil in a Dress', Alfonsina Strada learned to ride a bike at the age of 10 when her labourer father traded ten chickens for a battered old machine. With her powerful physique, bare legs and bobbed hair, Alfonsina had one ambition – to become a professional cyclist at a time – the 1920s – and in a place – post-war Italy – where opportunities to do so were almost zero.

But when the 1924 Giro d'Italia opened up the race to individual entrants (the trade teams were in dispute with race organisers over money and refused to ride, leaving the event without its stars), one Alfonsin Strada lined up in Milan and pinned the number 72 to 'his' jersey. Dropping the A to conceal her gender, Alfonsina Strada became the first – and so far only – woman to ride the Giro d'Italia. Forced to retire after a particularly torrid stage through the mountains of central Italy, Strada was allowed to continue in the race – the organisers paying for her food and lodgings and massage – and became a national heroine, with spectators waiting hours to catch a glimpse of her riding by. Often alone and in the dark, Strada rode every centimetre of the 3,613 km route. She continued her professional career, riding in the velodromes of Europe, beating male opponents and breaking records into her 40s. She died at the age of 69, crushed by her bright red 500cc Moto Guzzi motorbike after returning home from watching a bike race.
BLUFF FACT ▶ Alfonsina asked her husband for a racing bicycle for a wedding present.

T IS FOR ...

TOUR DE FRANCE

WHERE ▸ France, but the race occasionally starts in other countries and crosses the border into Spain and Italy for mountain stages.

TYPE OF RACE ▸ Stage race (three weeks), 21 stages with two rest days

STAGES ▸ Flat (sprints), mixed (breakaway), mountains (climbing specialists), time trial (specialists against the clock)

TIME OF YEAR ▸ July

MULTIPLE WINS ▸ Eddy Merckx, Miguel Indurain (the only rider to win five Tours in a row), Bernard Hinault and Jacques Anquetil

MOST WINS BY COUNTRY ▸ France

GREAT MOMENTS ▸ too many to mention but Eddy Merckx's solo attack in the Pyrenees in 1969; Hugo Koblet cementing his legend as the *Pedaleur de Charme* in 1951; Bartali's exploits to win a second Tour de France 10 years after his first in 1948; Coppi becoming the first ever winner on Alpe d'Huez in 1952; Anquetil and Poulidor ascending the Puy de Dome elbow to elbow in 1964; Fignon losing by a slender handful of seconds on the Champs-Élysées to LeMond in 1989; or Wiggins becoming the first-ever British winner in 2012.

JERSEYS ▸ Yellow jersey (winner), green jersey (points competition), white jersey with red polka dots (king of the mountains), white jersey (best young rider)

The Tour de France is the daddy of them all – the oldest and most famous stage race in the world. It's the one race every rider wants on their *palmarès* – be it a stage win, a jersey or standing on the podium in Paris as the overall winner. The Vuelta a España

CONTINUED OVERLEAF ▸

may be more challenging, the Giro might be the *aficionado*'s favourite but the Tour is the race that every rider in the world wants to ride in. It's the entry-level drug to the total addiction that is bike racing.

Founded in 1903 by Henri Desgrange *(see D)* and Géo Lefèvre to promote a newspaper, *l'Auto*, the Tour de France was the creation of a totally new sport – bicycle stage racing. Every aspect of modern-day cycle racing – from team time trialling to coloured jerseys, from the publicity caravan to mountain climbing – was pioneered by the Tour. That first race covered 2428 kilometres (1509 miles) in only six stages – the 100th Tour in 2013 covered 3404 kilometres (2115 miles) in 21 stages. There are strict rules now governing the length of stages, but back in Desgrange's day, riders would start at the crack of dawn and finish well after nightfall to cover distances up to 482 kilometres (1919 Tour, the longest stage ever).

Not surprisingly, Merckx holds many of the Tour records – most days in the yellow jersey, most stages won, greatest number of stages in a single Tour (eight, a record he shares with Charles Pélissier and Freddy Maertens) – but the Tour is about so much more than winners and statistics. It's about Eugene Christophe, the first man to wear the yellow jersey, running down a mountainside with his bike on his back to fix his broken forks at a local forge. It's about Jens Voigt riding 15 kilometres on a child's bike in a desperate attempt to stay in the race. It's about Honoré Barthélémy losing an eye when hit in the face by a flint and riding on to finish not just the stage but the race (he later said he spent more on replacement glass eyes than he made in prize money). It's about Eddy Merckx soloing to victory in the Pyrenees when the race was already won and Chris Froome riding to a famous victory in the yellow jersey on Mont Ventoux, Cavendish as imperious in the sprint as Pantani was on the climbs. It's about drama – the incidents that happen on and off the bike; the intense rivalries: Coppi–Bartali, LeMond–Hinault, Anquetil–Poulidor; the triumphs and disasters that face riders from minute to minute, hour to hour, day to day. It is utterly compelling and the only way to truly experience it is to get onto the roadside and experience the atmosphere as the peloton rushes past towards its destination.

> **BLUFF IT ▶** *'The Tour is great of course, but I prefer the Giro.'*

TANDEM

The 'bicycle built for two' was first patented in the 1890s at the height of the bicycle boom. Originally built by simply welding two bicycle frames together, the first modern tandem was designed by A.J. Wilson and Dan Albone in 1886. The word 'tandem' refers to the seating arrangement with riders sitting one behind the other – a bike where riders sit side by side is a 'sociable'.

But tandems weren't just for social riding, they were used for track racing too. From 1908 to 1972, tandem match sprinting was an Olympic event. Imagine two super-fast sprinters propelling a bike to speeds of up to 85 km/h. And now imagine the crashes ... But tandem track racing lives on at the Paralympic games where tandem pursuiting, time trialling and sprinting are alive and well on the track where a sighted 'pilot' works with a visually impaired 'stoker'.

TAYLOR Major

Marshall W. 'Major' Taylor was one of the first cycling superstars, coming to prominence during the first bicycle boom at the turn of the twentieth century. Born into poverty in Indianapolis, USA, in 1878, the grandson of a slave, he was virtually adopted by his father's employers and enjoyed all the privileges of a decent education and the freedom of the bicycle they gifted him. But when the family moved to Chicago, Taylor went from 'the happy life of a "millionaire kid" to that of a common errand boy', as he wrote in his autobiography *The Fastest Bicycle Rider in the World*. Hired by an Indianapolis bike shop in 1892 to perform stunts and tricks dressed in a military uniform, Taylor earned his nickname 'Major' and, at 14, started entering – and winning – races.

Smuggled into all-white races, Taylor's talent shone and, at 17, he was unofficially smashing world records held by professional cyclists. For all his talent, his audacity at crossing the colour bar earned him a ban from the Indianapolis track. But Major Taylor was on his way – in 1896 he competed for the first time in the hugely popular six-day races at Madison Square Gardens and the 'Black Cyclone', as he became known, was the leader of his own professional cycling team and the holder of seven world records before he turned twenty. In 1899 he became world champion.

But his colour saw him banned from races in the American South and threatened by spectators – who would throw ice and nails at him – and riders alike: one rival, unhappy at losing to Taylor, dragged him from his bike and choked him into unconsciousness. It was clear that the American would be better off riding in Europe, but Taylor initially refused to go and race in France. The major events were held on a Sunday, and the rider, whose deep religious convictions had been cemented by his mother's death, would not ride on the Sabbath. But the lure of rich pickings in Europe – and the willingness of race promoters to switch events from Sundays to French national holidays – saw Taylor cross the Atlantic in 1902 and take on allcomers, smashing the opposition and cementing his reputation as the fastest cyclist in the world.

But age was catching up with him and the American public's interest in bike racing was waning with the rise of the automobile. He retired in 1910 at the age of 32 and – after losing his fortune from a serious of poor investments – was reduced to hawking his self-published autobiography door to door in Chicago. When he died, at the age of 53, his body was unclaimed and he was buried in a pauper's grave.

But some of the sport's former stars still remembered the 'Black Cyclone' and the way he had lit up the tracks of the world. His remains were exhumed and reinterred in a properly marked grave with a bronze tablet bearing the inscription: 'World champion bicycle racer who came up the hard way – Without hatred in his heart – An honest, courageous and God-fearing, clean-living gentlemanly athlete. A credit to his race who always gave out his best— Gone but not forgotten.'

TECHNICAL

A mountain descent – or the run in to the finish of a race – that is particularly difficult to negotiate owing to switchbacks, sharp bends or road furniture *(see R)*.

TÊTE DE LA COURSE

YOU SAY ► *TET – D'LACK – ORSE*

WHAT IT MEANS ► Literally? Head of the race – it can refer to a solo rider, a small group, even the peloton. Whoever is leading the race is at the *tête de la course*.

TIFOSI

YOU SAY ► *TIFF – OH – SEE*

WHAT IT MEANS ► If you're a cycling fan in Italy – or you love Italian teams and riders – you're part of the *tifosi*: it's the Italian word for fan.

TIME TRIAL

Also known as the *contre-la-montre* or the race of truth, the principle is simple – you ride as fast as you can over a given distance and the rider who finishes in the quickest time wins. Riders start at timed intervals, usually one or two minutes, and are timed at checkpoints along the course and when they arrive at the finish line. They usually start in reverse order with the race leader going last. The short version is called a prologue and can't be any longer than eight kilometres. The team time trial involves all riders in a team starting together with the finish time being taken on the fifth rider to cross the line. The best time-trial teams ride in a strict formation called a chain gang or paceline *(see P)*, where each rider takes a turn to ride on the front for a set length of time ('taking a pull') then drops to the back of the formation. Jacques Anquetil, Miguel Indurain and Bradley Wiggins have all mastered the art of the winning races by dominating the time trial.

BLUFF FACT ► TI-Raleigh, the Netherlands-based team who dominated team time trialling in the 1970s and 1980s, were the first team to wear skinsuits, in the 1980 Tour de France, when they comfortably won both team time trials.

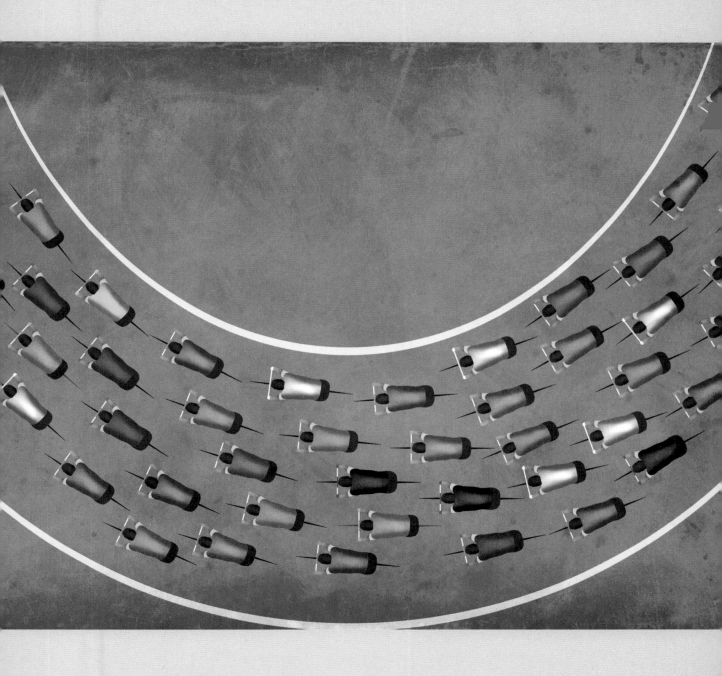

TOUR OF FLANDERS

WHERE ▶ Belgium (Flanders)

NICKNAME ▶ *Vlaanderens mooiste* (Dutch for 'Flanders' finest')

TYPE OF RACE ▶ One-day Classic

TERRAIN ▶ Cobbles and short, steep climbs like the Bosberg, Oude Kwaremont, Paterberg, Koppenberg and Muur van Geraardsbergen

TIME OF YEAR ▶ Spring, to be precise the 14th Sunday of the year

MULTIPLE WINS ▶ Achiel Buysse (Belgium), Fiorenzo Magni (Italy), Eric Leman (Belgium), Johan Museeuw (Belgium), Tom Boonen (Belgium), Fabian Cancellara (Switzerland) have all won the race three times

MOST WINS BY COUNTRY ▶ Belgium, of course

GREAT MOMENTS ▶ The Italian Fiorenzo Magni riding 75 kilometres alone to his third victory in 1951; Tom Simpson becoming the first Briton to ever win a Classic in 1961; Eddy Merckx winning by five and a half minutes in 1969; Tom Boonen winning Tour of Flanders and Paris–Roubaix in the same week in 2012 and Fabian Cancellara replicating the feat a year later.

The *Ronde van Vlaanderen* (to give it its proper name) was the creation of a newspaper, *Sportwereld*, and originally used the poorly finished cobbled roads of the region out of necessity. The sheer hard grind of those endless kilometres on punishing cobbles was what made the race so gruelling. In the 1920s and 1930s the inclusion of the coast road from Blankenberge to Oostend introduced another difficulty – the stiff coastal breezes that caused echelons in the peloton. Some of these stretches are still used in the race today. But the race is known for its cobbled climbs that toughen an already strenuous race into something truly remarkable. The Kwaremont came first in the early days of the race and is arguably the easiest of the bergs – it's longer and drags up more slowly than the short sharp shock of the Paterberg that follows. But as road surfaces improved in the 1960s and the old rough cobbles were replaced with asphalt, the *Ronde* looked towards the Ardennes and discovered the *hellingen* that have become the true backbone of the race. The Koppenberg hits the riders with a maximum gradient of 22 per cent, forcing all but the strongest to climb off their bike and run up the cobbles. Even the great Eddy Merckx was forced to walk up it in 1976. The Muur van Geraardsbergen may not be as tough as the Koppenberg but it is the place where the great winners have launched their decisive attacks. So steep that it can't be built on, for most of the year it's a pedestrianised zone leading up to the Ouderberg chapel. The locals have a saying: 'The Wall shall choose the winner.' However, with the finish line switching from Meerbeke to Oudenaarde in 2011, the Muur is no longer included in the race. But with or without it, the *Ronde* remains a Monument, whatever route it takes.

BLUFF IT ▶ *'Paris–Roubaix may be hell, but it doesn't have* hellingen' *(*hellingen *is the Dutch word for hills.)*

TOURMALET

ALTITUDE ► 2115 metres
HEIGHT GAIN ► 1275 metres
AVERAGE GRADIENT ► 7.5 per cent
MAXIMUM GRADIENT ► 11 per cent
LENGTH ► 17.1 kilometres
LOCATION ► French Pyrenees

The legend of how the Tour de France came to cross the Tourmalet, the highest peak in the central Pyrenees, is the story of Alphonse Steines, a journalist at *l'Auto* who pushed the race towards its heights. Convincing Henri Desgrange, the founder of the race, to let him reconnoitre the great mountain chain that separates France from Spain, he set off to assess the suitability of the Tourmalet. Steines envisaged a mountain stage the like of which no race had ever seen. He wanted to bring the Tour to the isolated region known as the 'Circle of Death', where bears lurked ready to pounce on the unwary and the tracks that passed for roads were virtually impassable, rock strewn and hazardous. He managed to drive to within four kilometres of the summit of the Tourmalet when he was trapped in a blizzard and was forced to abandon the car and struggle forward on foot. Wading through drifts chest deep as the snow continued to fall thickly, Steines finally made it over the summit and into the nearest town to be met by mountain guides and the local police. The next morning he sent a telegram to Desgrange. 'Crossed the Tourmalet. Stop. Very good road. Stop. Perfectly feasible. Stop. Signed Steines.' That piece of bravado is directly responsible for some of the most memorable images and stages in the Tour de France. Octave Lapize was the first rider to win a stage that crossed the Tourmalet in the 1910 Tour de France, the 326 km from Luchon to Bayonne. It took him 14 hours 10 minutes to cross the Peyresourde, Aspin, Tourmalet and Aubisque where he climbed off his bike and shouted 'Assassins!' at the commissaires following the race. Lapize who was the first rider ever to cross the summit of the Tourmalet and it is his steel statue, *le Géant*, that is towed to the summit on the first Saturday of the month each June. You can ride up alongside him as he makes his way annually to the top of the climb. He has good company – a bust of Jacques Goddet (race director from 1936–1986) shares the rarefied air at 2122 metres. There is no memorial to Alphonse Steines, the man who brought the Tour to the Tourmalet.

It was on the Tourmalet that one of the most famous of all the incidents in Tour history happened in 1913. Eugene Christophe broke his forks when he was hit by a car at the top of the climb, and was forced to descend 14 kilometres on foot, his bicycle on his back, to the village of Sainte-Marie-de-Campan. The rules decreed that he had to make all repairs himself, so he headed for the village forge and got to work, determined that his Peugeot team would finish with all eight riders in Paris. Christophe arrived three hours 50 minutes and 14 seconds behind the stage winner and was then penalised for allowing the blacksmith's son to work the bellows. It's said that the *commissaires* who were watching to see the rules were observed asked Christophe to get them something to eat. 'If you're hungry, eat coal!' the angry rider replied.

U IS FOR ...

UCI

The Union Cycliste International is the governing body of cycling. The UCI organise the world championships, rank events according to difficulty and award points for winning races for individuals, teams and countries. They are responsible for drawing up and enforcing the rules of various cycling disciplines which include road and track cycling, paracycling, mountain biking, cyclocross and BMX.

The UCI was first established to break the British dominance of the International Cycling Association (ICA) set up in 1892. At a meeting in Paris on 14 April, 1900, the national federations of France, Belgium, Italy, Switzerland and the United States set up what was to become the sport's new governing body. At the request of the International Olympic Committee (IOC) in 1965, the UCI split into two with a professional and an amateur organisation – the International Professional Cycling Federation (FICP) and the International Amateur Cycling Federation (FIAC) with the UCI acting as a coordinator. When the IOC dropped the amateur requirements for Olympic athletes in 1992, the FICP and the FIAC merged to create the UCI we know today.

If a nation wants to participate in UCI sanctioned events, then it must have a national federation to run the sport in that country. These national federations are grouped into five continental federations:

- Asian Cycling Confederation (ACC)
- Union Européenne de Cyclisme (UEC)
- Oceanian Cycling Confederation (OCC)
- Confederación Panamericana de Ciclismo (COPACI)
- Confédération Africaine de Cyclisme (CAC)

These five federations meet annually at the UCI Congress to discuss regulations and recognise new federations. The congress also elects the president

CONTINUED OVERLEAF ▶

and the nine members of the management committee who administer the sport.

In 2013, Britain's Brian Cookson was elected on a 'new broom' ticket as president after one of the darkest periods of the organisation's history. No stranger to controversy, the UCI has been led by a succession of characters who would give Sepp Blatter a run for his money – Spain's Luis Puig (President 1981–1990) presided over the controversy of the Pedro Delgado doping affair when the Spaniard escaped sanction for a failed drugs test at the Tour de France on a technicality and was succeeded by Hein Verbruggen (1991–2005) and Pat McQuaid (2005–2013), who were both heavily implicated in the US Postal doping conspiracy.

BLUFF FACT ▶ In 2013 OCC president Tracey Gaudry was elected as UCI vice-president, the highest office a woman has ever held in the organisation.

BLUFF IT ▶ *'Isn't it ironic how the UCI has come full circle? From trying to stop the Brits controlling the sport to having a Brit controlling the sport.'*

UNICYCLE

You wouldn't expect to see an acrobat in the Tour de France but then the unicycle is the only form of bicycle that we associate with the circus more than the street. No one knows quite when or why the unicycle developed, but the most popular theory is that penny farthing owners simply got rid of the little 'farthing' wheel and rode on the 'penny', with its pedals connected directly to the axle and seat positioned directly over the wheel exactly like the unicycle. Strangely enough, it was those thrill seekers in the extreme sports world that drove forward developments in the modern unicycle. First came the Muni (or mountain unicycle), with its fat, knobbly tyres like its cousin the mountain bike, and then the freestyle unicycle, adapted to do skateboard grinds and other tricks. There's even an International Unicycling Federation that organises unicycle racing, unicycle hockey and unicycle basketball.

BLUFF FACT ▶ All pupils at St Helen's School in Newbury, Ohio have to learn to unicycle.

V IS FOR ...

VOS Marianne

BORN ▶ 13 May, 1987, 's-Hertogenbosch, Netherlands
NATIONALITY ▶ Dutch
ACTIVE ▶ 2006–
NICKNAME ▶ Vosje, Little Fox
BIG WINS ▶ La Course (2014), gold medal Olympic road race (2012), 5 × UCI Women's Road World Cup (2007, 2009, 2010, 2012, 2013), 3 × Giro d'Italia Femminile (2011, 2012, 2014), 5 × Flèche Wallonne (2007, 2008, 2009, 2011, 2013), Tour of Flanders (2013), 7 × world cyclocross champion (2006, 2009, 2010, 2011, 2012, 2013, 2014), 2 × world track champion (2008, 2011), Olympic track gold medallist (2008)
MAJOR RIVALS ▶ None, she's head and shoulders above the rest

To put it simply, Marianne Vos is the female Eddy Merckx. She's head and shoulders above her rivals, the greatest rider of her generation. Born in 1987 at 's-Hertogenbosch, she was a natural athlete, swapping speed skating for mountain biking at 14. Vos is the complete all-rounder winning one-day Classics and stage races as well as competing on the track – where she's been world champion in the points and scratch events – and in cyclocross in the winter months. The Dutchwoman dominated the first ever Women's Tour, a British event first held in 2014, and won the first edition of La Course by Le Tour de France, the highest profile race on the women's calendar.

Vos also took the gold medal in the London Olympics in 2012, winning a thrilling sprint against Britain's Lizzie Armitstead on a rain-soaked Mall. It was the race that kick-started interest in the women's sport, and Vos has been active in the pressure group

CONTINUED OVERLEAF ▶

'Le Tour Entier', whose aim is to promote the women's sport and establish a women's Tour de France.

Vos started cycling at six, inspired by her elder brother Anton and was racing by the time she was eight, riding against – and often beating – the boys. Turning pro in 2004 after winning her first rainbow jersey, an unusual move for a woman cyclist, she decided to 'give it a go and try my best'. Vos initially found the pressure of her new found stardom difficult to cope with, but as her confidence grew she began to speak out as a passionate advocate for her sport.

Rapidly accumulating an astonishing series of results and winning every major women's race in the calendar, the Dutchwoman has dominated her sport since turning professional and is widely acknowledged as the one of the greatest cyclists of all time.

With a list of *palmarès* **(see P)** that would put most of the men's peloton to shame, Vos lists herself as a 'hobbycyclist' on her Facebook page and looks set to dominate her sport for years to come.

BLUFF IT ► *'It was no disgrace for Britain's Lizzie Armitstead to lose to Vos in the 2012 Olympic road race because Vos is the boss.'*

VELODROME

YOU SAY ► *VELL – A – DROME*

WHAT IS IT? ► Track cycling is the closest cycling gets to football or cricket – instead of the open road, it takes place on a wooden track in a purpose-built arena or velodrome. The word comes from the French, as so many cycling related terms do: vélo (bicycle) + drome (a racetrack). Early velodromes were often used for all kinds of sports, but cycling fans know them best for their steeply banked wooden cycling tracks – and a torrent of gold medals if you're a British cycling fan.

BLUFF IT ► *'The London Olympic velodrome is built from Siberian pine – produces the fastest surface, you know.'*

VENTOUX

YOU SAY ► *VON – TOO*
ALTITUDE ► 1909 metres
HEIGHT GAIN ► 1610 metres
AVERAGE GRADIENT ► 7.6 per cent
MAXIMUM GRADIENT ► 10.7 per cent
LENGTH ► 21 kilometres
LOCATION ► Provence, France

Mont Ventoux – also known as *Mont Chauve* or the Bald Mountain and the Giant of Provence – is a limestone mountain, part of the *massif des Cèdres* that rises above the lavender fields of the Provence region in Southern France. The gradient reaches 11 per cent *(see G for Gradient)* once the road climbs out of the tree line and onto the limestone scree slopes where ferocious winds have reached a maximum of 320 km/h (200 mph) – the word *venteux* means 'windy' in French – and they were strong enough in 2013 to blow down the solid granite slab of the Tom Simpson memorial. The French philosopher Roland Barthes called it 'the God of Evil' with customary hyperbole, but you can safely say that Mont Ventoux is a beast. There are harder climbs in cycling but none quite

so feared as the legendary Ventoux. When Eddy Merckx won there in 1970, he needed oxygen at the finish. Ferdi Kübler attacked at the foot of the climb in a heatwave in 1955, crashed several times, suffered heat stroke and announced his retirement that evening with the immortal words 'Ferdi has killed himself on the Ventoux!' On that same stage, French rider Jean Malléjac collapsed and lost consciousness for 15 minutes – it was a terrible omen of what was to come 12 years later.

It's most often used as a stage finish in the Tour de France and was first used as such in 1958 when Charly Gaul won the stage, though first climbed in 1951. Ventoux is also climbed in the Critérium du Dauphiné, one of the traditional warm-up races for the Tour. It has a mixed heritage for British cyclists: it's where Chris Froome sealed his victory in the 2013 race and where Tom Simpson died in 1967. There's a monument to him near the famous observatory on its barren, limestone slopes.

> **BLUFF IT** ► *'I'm a member of the Club des Cinglés, you know.' (The Club des Cinglés is for riders crazy enough to climb the Ventoux by all three routes in the space of 24 hours – you didn't do it, but they'll never know.)*

VICTORY SALUTE

When a rider crosses the line to win a race he usually raises his arms aloft in the traditional V of victory. But there have been some memorable salutes over the years including Carlos Sastre sucking his daughter's dummy and Mark Cavendish sticking two fingers up at his critics. Perhaps the strangest victory salute was

Filippo Simeoni's when he dismounted before the finish and carried his bike over the line.

BLUFF FACT ► Alberto Contador has trademarked his fingerbang 'pistolero' salute and it appears on a range of merchandise.

> **BLUFF IT** ► *'You have to love Juan Antonio Flecha's bow firing salute' (Flecha is the Spanish word for arrow)*

VIRENQUE Richard

BORN ▸ 19 November, 1969, Casablanca, Morocco
NATIONALITY ▸ French
ACTIVE ▸ 1991–2004
RIDER TYPE ▸ Climbing specialist
NICKNAME ▸ Ricco
BIG WINS ▸ 7 × king of the mountains polka dot jersey, Tour de France (1994, 1995, 1996, 1997, 1999, 2003, 2004), Paris–Tours (2001)
MAJOR RIVAL ▸ Marco Pantani

Richard Virenque is, on paper, the greatest climber ever to race the Tour de France winning a record seven king of the mountain jerseys. Yet the Frenchman, who was known for his long-range attacks in which he would snaffle as many mountain points as possible, is now almost universally reviled by cycling fans for his part in the Festina Affair *(see F)* and is one of the sport's great pantomime villains for his perceived arrogance and failure to admit to doping. He remains popular in his homeland, however, where he now works as a commentator for French Eurosport.

When Virenque surpassed both Lucien Van Impe and Federico Bahamontes's record of six king of the mountains wins in 2004, Van Impe criticised him for being opportunistic, saying he himself hadn't wanted to break Bahamontes's record six wins out of respect for the great Spaniard. Bahamontes weighed in, saying it was a shame that Virenque was now regarded as the greatest climber as he didn't have the ability to contest for the overall at the Tour – both Bahamontes (1959) and Van Impe (1976) had also taken that ultimate prize, the yellow jersey.

Bahamontes's criticism – that Virenque was never a contender for overall honours and was allowed to take the king of the mountains precisely because he was no threat – is not entirely fair, though it became so towards the end of the Frenchman's career, a reflection of the way the sport had become more specialised. No longer does the points or the mountains classification go to a rider in contention for overall honours. But with the support of the Festina team, Virenque was most certainly a contender, capable not only of beating the best climbers like Pantani *(see P)*, as he did by four minutes in a monstrous day in the Pyrenees in 1994, but also of finishing on the podium which he did twice in the Tour de France, finishing third in 1996 and second in 1997. In what was his best performance in his home Tour, the Frenchman took a fantastic win at Courchevel, outsprinting Jan Ullrich after a typically attacking ride and a performance by his Festina team on the climbs that set the blueprint for the Armstrong years. Then, on a seemingly innocuous stage in the Vosges mountains, Virenque genuinely had Ullrich on the ropes. The Frenchman was a fearless descender, to the point of madness, the German was not. But Pantani refused to work with Virenque and the opportunity was lost. It later emerged that Virenque had offered to pay Ullrich 100,000 francs to let him win the stage then offered Pantani 10,000 francs to help him try and win the Tour. It was yet more scandal heaped on Virenque's head, though buying and selling races is as old as the sport itself.

Virenque cried when he and his team were ejected from the Tour the following year, then wriggled onto the hook of doping accusations claiming he was doped without his consent, for which he was widely pilloried in the French media. He was finally banned at the end of the 2000 season when he admitted to doping in court. But not before he'd added the 1999 king of the mountains jersey and a stage win in 2000 to his *palmarès (see P)*. He came back to the Tour in 2002, taking a stage win on Mont Ventoux and two more polka dot jerseys before he retired in 2004. His last hurrah was a stage win in Saint-Flour in his final Tour de France. On Bastille Day, 14 July, he attacked on the first of the nine climbs of the day and crossed the line alone after a 204 km breakaway, assuring himself of a notable stage win reminiscent of his early raids in the Alps and Pyrenees and a final, historic polka dot jersey.

BLUFF FACT ▶ In 2006 Virenque won the French version of 'I'm a Celebrity ...' *('Je suis une célébrité, sortez-moi de là!')* proving that his reputation as the 'French housewife's favourite' remains intact.

BLUFF IT ▶ *'There's a rock band from Spain called Virenque – not Indurain, Virenque.'*

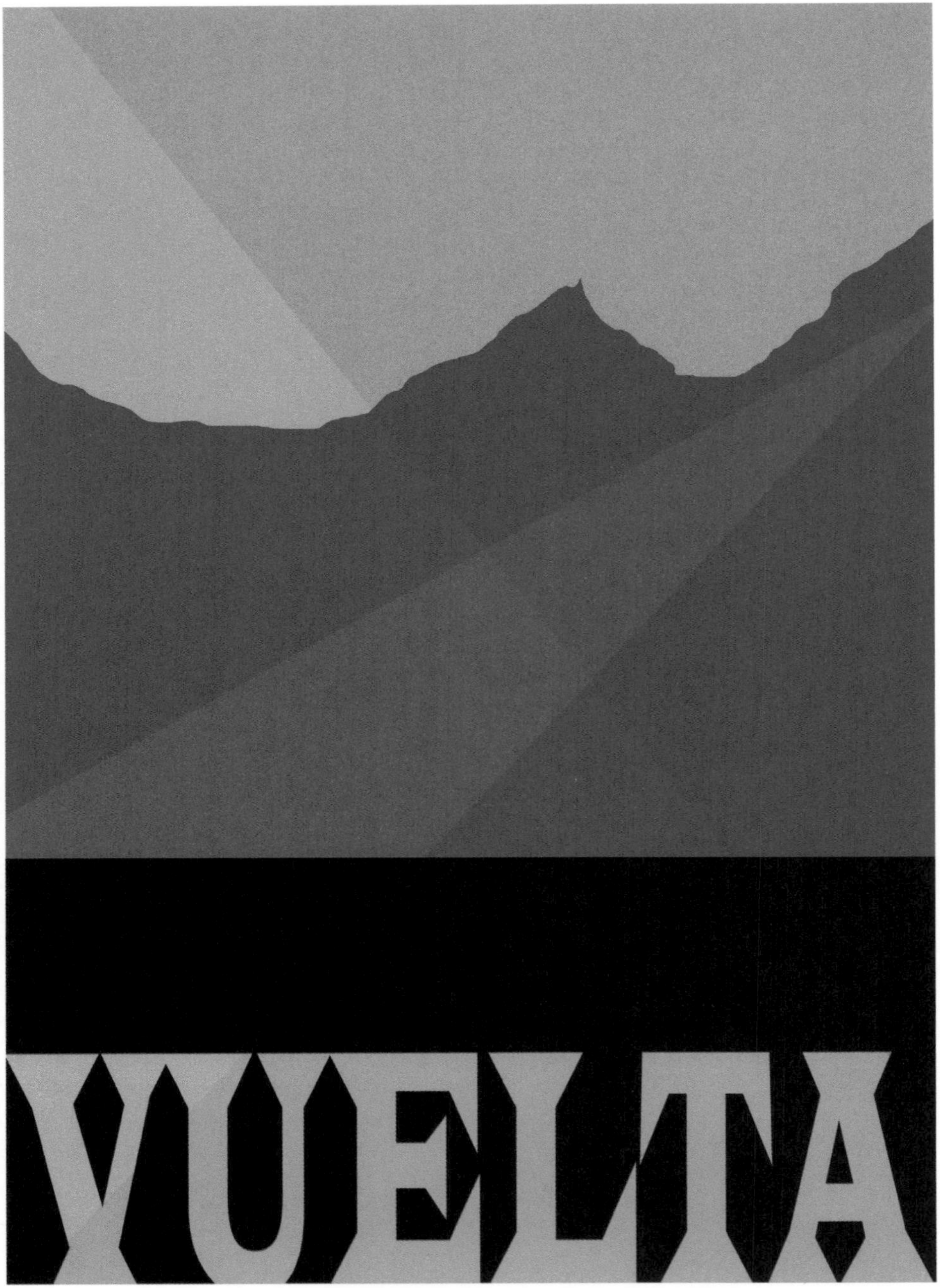
VUELTA

VUELTA A ESPAÑA

YOU SAY ▸ *BWELL (as in all but the first two letters of 'rub well') –TA (or more often in English 'VWELL – TA') UH (as in huh) ES – PAN – YA*

WHERE ▸ Spain

TYPE OF RACE ▸ Stage race (three weeks), 21 stages with two rest days

STAGES ▸ Flat (sprints), mixed (breakaway), mountains (climbing specialists), time trial (specialists against the clock)

TIME OF YEAR ▸ September

MULTIPLE WINS ▸ Tony Rominger (Swiss) and Roberto Heras (Spain) have each won three times

MOST WINS BY COUNTRY ▸ Spain

GREAT MOMENTS ▸ Freddy Maertens winning 13 stages in 1977, the most ever in a Grand Tour, on his way to winning the race overall and the points jersey; Éric Caritoux winning by just six seconds in 1984, the smallest winning margin in any Grand Tour; Chris Horner winning in 2013 to become the oldest winner of any Grand Tour – he was 41.

JERSEYS ▸ Red jersey (winner), green jersey (points competition), white jersey with blue polka dots (king of the mountains), white jersey (best young rider)

WHAT IS IT? ▸ The Vuelta is the baby brother of the three Grand Tours, started in 1935 by a newspaper, the *Diario Internacionales*, to showcase the countryside of Spain. The first Vuelta covered 3425 miles in 14 stages and was won by a Belgian, Gustaaf Deloor. But the outbreak of civil war in Spain followed by the Second World War meant that the race didn't really find its feet until 1955, but it's been run ever since, switching from its traditional April start to September in 1995 to avoid a conflict with the Giro d'Italia in May.

The Vuelta has a reputation as a climbers' race and features some of the hardest mountains in any of the three Grand Tours, including the fearsome Angliru, the toughest part of which is known simply as 'the goat track' because that's exactly what it is. It's so tough that even the best climbers have been known to come to a grinding halt on its steepest sections. Britain's David Millar crashed three times on the ascent in 2008 and retired from the race in protest, climbing off his bike and removing his race number 500 metres from the finish line. The Vuelta also climbed the Angliru in 2011, which saw Chris Froome's breakout Grand Tour performance when he and Sir Bradley Wiggins finished second and third respectively, the best finish by British riders in the race since Robert Millar, the Scottish climber, finished second in 1985. Millar fell victim to what the French sports paper *l'Équipe* called 'a formidable Spanish coalition' of teams working against him. Ireland's Sean Kelly had better luck in 1988, when he won the race overall and took the points classification for the fourth time.

The Vuelta tends to stay inside Spanish borders – and why wouldn't it? From the lush green of the Basque country to the heights of the Pyrenees, across the barren plains of the southeast to the glorious beaches of the *Costa de la Luz*, Spain has every type of challenging terrain that a bike race requires.

BLUFF IT ▸ *'Did you know the 2013 winner Chris Horner is the oldest ever winner of a Grand Tour? At 41 he's five years older than Firmin Lambot who won the 1922 Tour de France aged 36.'*

W IS FOR ...

WIGGINS Sir Bradley

BORN ▶ April 28, 1980, Ghent, Belgium
NATIONALITY ▶ British
ACTIVE ▶ 2001–
RIDER TYPE ▶ Track and road, time-trial specialist
NICKNAME ▶ Wiggo
BIG WINS ▶ Tour de France (2012), Olympic time trial (2012), 6 × world championship track gold medals (2003, 2007, 2008), 3 × Olympic track gold medals (2004, 2008)
RIVAL ▶ Chris Froome

Sir Bradley Marc Wiggins is that rare rider – one who excels on the track as well as the road. In the modern era of specialisation, where riders focus on the Classics or the Grand Tours or the track, Wiggins has ridden in all these disciplines with great success as his *palmarès (see P)* show.

The son of a professional cyclist, he was born in Belgium but grew up in Kilburn, London and started cycling at 12, inspired by the success of Chris Boardman in the 1992 Olympics. Telling one of his school teachers he was going to be a cyclist and win Olympic gold and the yellow jersey, he found early success on the track, becoming junior world pursuit champion at 18. Further success on the track followed – Wiggins is Great Britain's most decorated Olympian with seven medals – but his breakthrough on the road didn't come until he was 29 when, riding for the American Garmin team, he finished fourth at the 2009 Tour de France (the official result now credits him with a third place owing to the disqualification of Lance Armstrong). But it was three years later when, riding for Britain's Team Sky, Wiggins became

CONTINUED OVERLEAF ▶

the first ever Briton to stand on top of the podium in the Tour de France and made good on his boyhood prediction.

Known as 'the fastest mod on two wheels', the cycling Sir is a huge fan of Paul Weller, sharp suits and sideburns. When asked about his career he said, 'It's the stuff of dreams ... As a child, being a fan of the sport, I never imagined that one day I'd be in this position. Kids from Kilburn don't become favourite for the Tour de France. You're supposed to become a postman or a milkman or work in Ladbrokes.' Ladbrokes' loss has most definitely been cycling's gain, and he's not done yet. Wiggins hopes to finish his career with yet another gold medal at the Rio Olympics in 2016.

In 2015, Wiggins broke the Hour record in London to set a mark of 54.526km, beating the old record by a massive 1.5km. He joins an elite club of riders – Coppi, Anquetil, Merckx and Indurain – who have won the Tour de France and held the Hour record.

BLUFF FACT ▶ Wiggin's father Gary used to smuggle amphetamines through customs in his baby son's nappies, an act which made his son vehemently anti-doping. Gary Wiggins died in mysterious circumstances after a brawl at a party in his native Australia in 2008.

> **BLUFF IT** ▶ *'When he appeared on Desert Island Discs in 2015, Wiggo chose David Bowie's 'Sound & Vision' as his favourite track and a family photograph album as his luxury – awww'*

WHEELSUCKER

These are the riders you see in a breakaway with their nose glued to the rear wheel of the rider in front. The polite term is 'drafting' or 'sitting in', and it saves the rider behind about 20 per cent in terms of energy used as they benefit from being shielded by the body in front. Laurent Fignon famously called Greg LeMond a wheelsucker in the 1989 Tour de France. Fignon was an attacking rider while LeMond was more calculating and tended to follow behind his adversary. Drafting is a legitimate tactic but no rider likes to be known as someone who can only follow the wheels and never take a turn on the front. The bottom line: the wheelsucker is that annoying [insert insult here] who sits on your back wheel and then beats you in a sprint. Nobody likes a wheelsucker so try not to be one.

It's what every cyclist aspires to do - from the local time trial to the Tour de France, every rider wants to stand on the top step of the podium. After winning his first ever race the great Eddy Merckx cried "I've won! Now I don't have to go to school anymore!" But for others winning has not been so sweet – Sir Bradley Wiggins has spoken openly about how much he hated being the winner of the 2012 Tour de France and how he spiralled into depression as a result. And Lance Armstrong has admitted that taking the 'win at all costs' attitude he developed in his fight against cancer into his cycling career led directly to his doping.

> **BLUFF IT** ▶ *'As Mario Cipollini said "if you're braking, you're not winning."*

WHEELSUCKER

53x11

X IS FOR...

X IS FOR ...

53 × 11

Or 25 × 11 or 29 × 12 or any of the many gear ratios that professional cyclists use when they're racing. 53 × 11 is the common highest gear ratio found on road bikes. Put very simply, the better the cyclist you are, the bigger the gear ratio you can use.

It works like this: the reason bikes have gears is that, if they didn't, we'd still be riding penny farthings. If you have a front chainring with 42 teeth and a rear sprocket with 14 teeth you have a 3:1 gear ratio (3 × 14 = 42) which means that for each full pedal stroke your wheel makes three full revolutions. Which means your *actual* back wheel can be much smaller – the size of a regular bike wheel in fact, around 26 inches – because your *imaginary* bike wheel is 78 inches. And smaller equals safer.

The idea behind having multiple gears is that it allows you to move your bike forward a different distance with every pedal stroke. A low gear is ideal for climbing those hills and pretending you're Chris Froome effortlessly pedalling away from the rest on Mont Ventoux. In a medium gear you'll be able to ride at mid-speed for miles, channelling your inner Bradley Wiggins. Put your bike in the biggest possible gear and you'll be flying like Cav.

One word of caution – never use the smallest chainring with the smallest sprocket, or the biggest chainring with the biggest sprocket. You'll stretch your chain and wear it out quicker than you can say 53 × 11.

> **BLUFF IT ▶** *'Can't believe you're in your granny gear!' (Said laughingly as you fly past your rival in your biggest gear – the 'granny gear' uses the smallest front ring and the biggest rear cog and is so called because it's supposed to be the gear little old ladies use when they're out for a spin.)*

Y IS FOR ...

YELLOW JERSEY

The biggest prize in cycling, the yellow jersey – or *maillot jaune* in French – was introduced to the Tour de France in 1919. It happened like this: although individual bike manufacturers had supported teams in the race since 1909, because of the lack of resources to support individual teams after the First World War all the riders in the 1919 Tour rode for a conglomerate La Sportive team, in uniform grey jerseys with their team allegiances denoted by different coloured epaulettes – purple for Peugeot, dark green for Automoto, blue for Alcyon and so on. Alphonse Baugé, *directeur sportif (see D)* for Peugeot and then Alcyon, had already experimented with dressing his team personnel in yellow so that his riders could pick them out more easily at the road side. A light bulb went on in Baugé's head – why not distinguish the leader of the race with a distinctive jersey? And what better colour than yellow – not only highly visible, but also the colour of the pages that the newspaper *l'Auto* – that sponsored the race – was printed on? The first rider to wear it was Eugene Christophe, though he would never wear it all the way to Paris as the overall winner. Eddy Merckx has worn it more than any other rider, though he never wore it from start to finish in the race – only three riders have achieved that feat: Ottavio Bottecchia (1924), Nicolas Frantz (1928) and Romain Maes (1935). Fabian Cancellara holds the record for wearing the most yellow jerseys without ever winning the race – 28 of them.

In 1947 Louison Bobet refused to wear the yellow jersey. The reason? It was sponsored by Sofil, manufacturers of artificial yarn and Bobet refused to wear anything but wool (he suffered with a terrible skin complaint and said wool was more hygienic). No compromise could be reached and Sofil were forced to make Bobet a woollen jersey.

As with most Tour-related tales, there is another version of the birth of the yellow jersey. This says that yellow jerseys were the only ones available in any quantity in post-war France – yellow was an unpopular colour, possibly for its associations with cowardice.

BLUFF FACT ▶ The yellow jersey used to have the initials H. D. on the left breast – these initials stand for Henri Desgrange, the 'Father of the Tour'.

BLUFF FACT ▶ Philippe Thys, who won the Tour de France in 1913, 1914 and 1920 and was known as 'the Basset Hound' for his low-slung riding style, always claimed that he was the first rider to be asked to wear a yellow jersey at the Tour. He claimed Baugé had asked him to wear it in 1914, but he'd refused as the other riders called him a canary.

> **BLUFF IT** ▶ *'The yellow jersey that the leader receives each day opens down the back, a bit like a hospital gown – makes it easier for the podium girls to put it on the rider quickly – after all who'd want to get too close to a cyclist's armpits after they've spent six hours in the saddle?'*

Z IS FOR ...

ZONCOLAN

YOU SAY ▸ *ZONG – CO – LAN*

ALTITUDE ▸ 1750 metres

HEIGHT GAIN ▸ 1210 metres

AVERAGE GRADIENT ▸ 11.5 per cent

MAXIMUM GRADIENT ▸ 20 per cent

LENGTH ▸ 10.5 kilometres

LOCATION ▸ Italian Alps

There's a banner that hangs across the road at the foot of the Zoncolan. It says *'la porta per l'inferno'* (the gate of hell), and though the first kilometres seem deceptively easy, as the climb grinds relentlessly onwards and upwards on the poorly surfaced roads, it seems ever more truthful. The Zoncolan has become as mythical as the Alpe d'Huez or the Galibier or the Angliru, yet it was only discovered by the Giro d'Italia in 2003 and has been used only a handful of times since. The climb is almost too hard, with most riders barely able to do more than push the pedals round as they struggle to the top. Only the pure climbers have any hopes of stamping decisively on the pedals and launching an attack, especially since over the final six kilometres of the climb the gradient rises to an average 15 per cent.

BLUFF IT ▸ *'Fabiana Luperini won a stage finish here in the women's Giro in 1997 – that's six years before the men's Giro tackled the climb.'*

ZABEL Erik

BORN ▸ 7 July, 1970, East Berlin, Germany
NATIONALITY ▸ German
RIDER TYPE ▸ Sprinter
ACTIVE ▸ 1993–2008
NICKNAMES ▸ Ete, Mr Milan–San Remo
BIG WINS ▸ 6 × green jersey, Tour de France (1996–2001); 3 × points jersey, Vuelta a España (2002–2004); 4 × Milan–San Remo (1997, 1998, 2000, 2001)
MAJOR RIVALS ▸ Stuart O'Grady, Mario Cipollini, Laurent Jalabert, Robbie McEwen

Germany's Erik Zabel is one of the greatest sprinters of all time, and has won more points jerseys than any other rider, dominating the green jersey competition at the Tour in the 1990s by taking six straight victories.

After a series of good amateur results, Zabel joined the German powerhouse team Team Telekom (later T-Mobile), who, along with the French Festina team, would be the strongest squads in the Grand Tours in the 1990s. Telekom were utterly dominant in the 1996 Tour de France with Bjarne Riis becoming the first ever Danish winner and Germany's Jan Ullrich taking the best young rider competition to go with Zabel's green jersey. The next year they went one better – along with Ullrich becoming the first ever German winner of the Tour at the age of 23 (his winning margin of nine minutes and nine seconds was the biggest since 1984 and his victory in both the overall and best young rider classifications was the first since Laurent Fignon achieved the feat in 1983), Telekom were the best team and Zabel once again carried the green jersey to Paris.

It was the German's ability to get over the mountains as well as unleash a ferocious sprint that made him so unstoppable. Where rivals like Mario Cipollini would climb off at the first sight of the Alps or Pyrenees, Zabel could weather the climbs and make it through to the end of the race. The German was never a pure stage-winning machine like Italian Mario Cipollini or Britain's Mark Cavendish and not always the fastest sprinter, but what Zabel lacked in sheer speed he made up for in consistency, picking up points for repeatedly placing highly on stages. In fact he won the points classification in 1998 and 1999 without winning a stage, prompting one of his rivals, Australia's Robbie McEwen, to demand that the rules be changed so that the green jersey could only be awarded if the rider taking it to Paris had won a stage.

Consistency, climbing ability, tactical astuteness – these were the qualities that netted him so many points jerseys, including a memorable battle with Australia's Stuart O'Grady in 2001, the last year of his remarkable run. O'Grady had held the green jersey for eleven stages with the German nibbling away at his lead – going into the final stage on the Champs-Élysées, Zabel was only two points behind. The Czech sprinter Ján Svorada took the coveted stage win, but Zabel's second place ahead of O'Grady in third gave him his final green jersey by eight points. It was all the greater an achievement because his team had sent him to the race without his favoured leadout man, the Italian Gian Matteo Fagnini and it was Zabel's ability to get on the right wheel for the sprint that helped him to three stage wins that year.

After retirement, Zabel continued to be active in

CONTINUED OVERLEAF ▸

the sport and guided Britain's Mark Cavendish to the centenary win at Milan–San Remo, a race he had won four times in his career.

But Zabel's greatest successes were achieved in one of the darkest periods of the sport and the German wasn't immune from its doping culture. In 2013 he finally admitted to the sueddeutsche.de website that he had used EPO, cortisone and blood doping from 1996 to 2003.

BLUFF FACT ▶ In 2004, Zabel started his season by losing what would have been his fifth Milan–San Remo in a bizarre fashion – he started celebrating too soon, allowing Spain's Oscar Freire to sneak past him for the win. He ended the season by coming second in the world road race championship, beaten again by Oscar Freire.

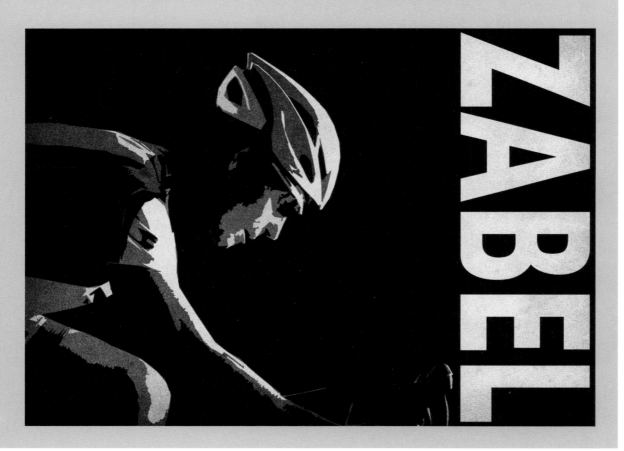

ZOETEMELK Joop

BORN ▶ 3 December , 1946, Rijpwetering, Netherlands

NATIONALITY ▶ Dutch

ACTIVE ▶ 1970–1987

RIDER TYPE ▶ All-rounder

NICKNAMES ▶ Joop, the Wheelsucker (so called by Eddy Merckx for his prolific number of second place finishes), the Most French Dutchman (he rode for a string of French teams – Mercier, Gitane and LeJeune – and made his home in France, running a hotel in Meaux in the île de France), the Dutchman of the Tour

BIG WINS ▶ Tour de France (1980), Vuelta a España (1979), world road champion (1985), Paris–Nice (1974, 1975, 1979), Paris–Tours (1977, 1979)

MAJOR RIVALS ▶ Eddy Merckx, Bernard Hinault

In any other era Hendrik Gerardus Jozef Zoetemelk, known as Joop, would have won many more races than he did, but he started his career during the Merckx era and ended it during Hinault's, arguably the two greatest riders of all time.

Naturally pale, the joke was that Zoetemelk never tanned because he was always in Merckx's shadow. Everyone who worked with him was quick to praise his temperament, it was said of him: 'He followed the rules, he got on with people. He never asked for *domestiques*. Joop never demanded anything.' But it's for his extraordinary record at the Tour de France that Zoetemelk is best remembered – in a record 16 appearances at the race, he never finished lower than 30th and between 1970 and 1982 he never finished lower than eighth. He was second six times in that period and finally won in 1980, riding for the Dutch TI-Raleigh team. A complete rider, Zoetemelk also scored victories in races like Paris–Nice and the Amstel Gold as well as being Dutch national champion. He finally won the world road race championship at the age of 38, making him the oldest rider ever to wear the rainbow jersey *(see R)*.

But Zoetemelk had a dark secret – his French wife Françoise was an alcoholic. Zoetemelk himself said: 'I later told my father-in-law that if I hadn't become involved with his family my career would have been much more successful as a rider.' Unable to confide in anyone, not even his sister, Zoetemelk became more and more withdrawn. Team-mates said he turned from one of the boys into an increasingly remote and inward-looking figure as he struggled to cope with his wife's erratic behaviour and bring up their two children – his son Karl became a French mountain bike champion.

The Dutch cycling federation named him the greatest Dutch rider of all time and there is a Joop Zoetemelk Classic race every March which passes the statue of him at Rijpwetering, where he was born and grew up.

BLUFF IT ▶ *'Joop Zoetemelk was the first man to wear the polka dot jersey as king of the mountains in 1975.'*

ACKNOWLEDGEMENTS

Suze Clemitson

To my brilliant family – Paul my lovely husband, Tom my shining son and Jan my wonderful mum – my eternal thanks for giving me the love, time, support and unquestioning faith to pursue my dream of putting words on paper. And to my brother for asking me all the tough but necessary questions.

To Charlotte and Sarah and all the team at Bloomsbury for taking those words and turning them into this book – it's been a steep learning curve but an endlessly fascinating and enjoyable one.

To Mr Mark Fairhurst for being a dream collaborator and providing the perfect images.

To my Twitter friends who contributed thoughts and ideas for cycling terminology from A–Z and continue to be a source of information, knowledge and great gossip.

To Lucy who held my hand through it all over cups of coffee and longs walks, where she helped me get the whole process straight in my head. And for Ned and Kathy who did more of the same through transatlantic emails.

To Rory Scarfe and Don McRae for all the mentoring and support.

To Scott and John at the Velocast for keeping me going through the tough times and much more.

Finally to my dear, dead dad who drove me to far-flung places and sat with me by the roads of France, reading a Maigret, whilst the Tour went by. I promised you a book and this, finally, is the one I've written.

Mark Fairhurst

Much love and thanks to Heidi who has been a constant source of encouragement and direction in producing my artworks. Zeitgeist Images wouldn't work without her!

I must also thank Suze Clemitson for entrusting me to illustrate this book, Sir Dave Brailsford for the foreward, Charlotte Croft and Sarah Cole of Bloomsbury, and lastly, my followers on Twitter.